Managing
Business
Transactions

Managing Business Transactions

Controlling the Cost of Coordinating, Communicating, and Decision Making

Paul H. Rubin

Foreword by
Oliver E. Williamson

THE FREE PRESS
A Division of Macmillan, Inc.
NEW YORK

Collier Macmillan Canada
TORONTO

Maxwell Macmillan International
NEW YORK   OXFORD   SINGAPORE   SYDNEY

The Free Press
A Division of Macmillan, Inc.
866 Third Avenue, New York, N.Y. 10022

Collier Macmillan Canada, Inc.
1200 Eglinton Avenue East
Suite 200
Don Mills, Ontario M3C 3N1

Printed in the United States of America

printing number

1 2 3 4 5 6 7 8 9 10

Library of Congress Cataloging-in-Publication Data

Rubin, Paul H.
  Managing business transactions: controlling the cost of coordinating, communicating, and decision making/Paul H. Rubin; Foreword by Oliver E. Williamson.
       p.   cm.
  ISBN   0-02-927595-4
   1. Managerial economics. 2. Contracts. 3. Related party transactions. 4. Transaction costs. 5. Negotiation in business. 6. Law—Economic aspects—United States.   I. Title.
HD30.22.R82   1990
658.15′52—dc20   90-34270
                                                       CIP

*To my wife, Martie Moss,
for faith and encouragement*

Contents

Foreword by Oliver E. Williamson   ix
Preface and Acknowledgments   xi

PART I *Inputs*   1

1 *Make or Buy?*   3
2 *Buying Complex Products*   23
3 *Structuring Employment Agreements*   47

PART II *Capital and Finance*   71

4 *Some Notes on Finance*   73
5 *Takeovers and Restructurings*   94

PART III *Marketing*   115

6 *Distributing the Product: Vertical Controls*   117
7 *Franchising*   134
8 *Creating a Reputation*   145
   Summary and Implications   162

   Glossary   167
   Bibliography   173
   Index   175

Foreword

What Paul Rubin refers to as "transaction management" draws on, integrates, and interprets recent work in "law and economics," "industrial organization," and, especially, "transaction cost economics." As is apparent from his discussion, this work has considerable relevance for business lawyers and business managers. That its operational significance is only now being realized is largely because most of the work is very recent, much of it having appeared only in the past ten and twenty years, and because most of it has been published in specialized journals and books.

Managing Business Transactions is the first book-length treatment of the new economics of organization that makes this scholarship accessible and meaningful to an audience of nonspecialists. That is a very considerable achievement. New ways of thinking about organization and the public policy ramifications that accrue thereto leave readers with a deeper and broader understanding of what modern business enterprise is all about.

Contrary to earlier scholarship, which held that organizational variety had monopoly purpose and effect, the new scholarship regards monopoly as a special case and adopts an economizing orientation instead. Rather, therefore, than view the economics of organization through a lens peculiar to monopoly theory, the new scholarship is expressly concerned instead with core problems of organization. Here, as elsewhere, it takes a theory to beat a theory—and for a long time the monopoly theory was the only game in town. A new logic of organization needed to be crafted.

Not only did a new logic have to be developed, but it needed to make its way against orthodoxy. Within the transactional domain, the new theory is more genuine. It furthermore appeals to the intuition of experienced practitioners by formulating in language what business-men, lawyers, politicians, and others "could feel but could not tell."

Much of the material in this book is associated with the "new institutional economics," which has been described by one leading economist as "one of the liveliest areas in our discipline." That it is referred to as "new" is both because it is recent and because it is to be distinguished from an older variety of institutional economics that fell on hard times for failure to address real issues in an operational way. That it is "institutional" is because institutions are perceived to play key and hitherto neglected roles in a high-performance economy. That it is referred to as "economics" is because economizing is held to be the main purpose, albeit not the exclusive purpose, of economic organization.

Straight thinking about economic organization requires an appreciation for economic institutions, a willingness to plumb the details of contract and organization that lawyers and economists had tended previously to gloss over, and an appreciation for the extraordinary power and reach of the economizing approach. As Rubin's book makes clear, our understanding of a huge number of production, employment, financial, and marketing issues has been reshaped as a consequence.

Indeed, any issue that can be posed directly or indirectly as a contracting issue can be addressed to advantage in "transaction management" terms. Many issues, of which the mundane make-or-buy decision is a prototypical example, arise naturally in contracting terms. What occasions continuing surprise is that a large number of issues which appear to lack a contracting structure can be reformulated to advantage in contracting terms—for example, the cartel problem, the organization of golf clubs, and the company town. One of the joys of this approach is that applications are endless once a threshold level of "transaction management" understanding has been crossed. That warrants the following precaution: Readers who reach this level of understanding are warned that their way of thinking about complex organizations will thereafter be permanently altered.

OLIVER E. WILLIAMSON

Preface and Acknowledgments

- In order to avoid a hostile takeover, a group of senior managers of a firm undertakes a leveraged buyout.
- A firm must decide between issuing stock and borrowing in order to obtain $50 million in financing for a new project.
- One firm makes a hostile offer for another because the first thinks it can do a better job of managing the assets.
- A defense contractor orders a customized machine which is absolutely essential for the successful completion of a contract.
- A specialized consultant is needed to purchase and set up a firm's computer system, and a method of compensation must be devised.
- A successful fried chicken restaurant wants to sell franchises. It wants to structure its program so that its franchisees will provide the right amount of advertising and quality.
- A high-quality firm in a business full of fly-by-night operators wants to be able to convince consumers of its quality.
- A firm needs a steady supply of highly specialized machined parts, and must decide if it should make them or buy them.
- The vice-president for marketing wants the vice-president for production to change the specifications on a product.
- A firm manufacturing a complex product, like a home computer, wants its distributors to demonstrate the use of the machine.
- A purchasing agent places an order for five reams of standardized copying paper of a given size and quality with a local office supply store.

This is a list of transactions. The last is a *simple* transaction: buying of a given grade of material from a known supplier when the product is readily available from many other sources. All the rest of the transactions are *complex* because they involve terms other than simple price and quantity. Some are transactions relating to the essence of the firm, its ownership and organization. In some of them, the buyer is uncertain about exactly what it is buying. In some, there will be an ongoing relationship between buyers and sellers after the purchase is made. In some, there is only one seller of a specialized input. In most cases, one party to the transaction knows more than the other, and the less knowledgeable party does not want to be exploited because of his ignorance.

In all cases, it is important to devise terms of the transactions which will provide proper incentives for both parties. In many cases, if the terms of the transaction are incorrect, the firm may fail. Even if less is at stake, correct structuring of these transactions can greatly increase the profits of the firm and make the lives of managers much more pleasant. If proper structuring of transactions can avoid a hostile takeover, jobs of managers can be saved.

An important part of the job of managing is the structuring and management of complex transactions. Transactions like the last in the list of examples are simple and can be handled routinely through the purchasing department. But all of the others require active management. Moreover, managers in any part of the firm might be involved in these complex exchanges. It is not possible to limit their scope to one division (such as the purchasing division). The examples mentioned above would include managers involved in production, personnel, finance, marketing, and purchasing. Managers at all levels, from foreman to top executive or even board member, are also involved in these transactions, and should understand ways of managing them.

In addition, as one of the examples indicates, some of the transactions involved will be within a firm, rather than between firms. For a complex organization such as a modern large corporation, there will be many within-firm transactions, and even in these transactions, the various parties will not necessarily have the same goals. For example, the production department may be charged a price for an input made by a subdivision, and this charge may be reflected in the earnings of the subdivision. Then the subdivision will want this charge to be as high as possible, while the production department will want it to be low. While employees of the same firm may limit the amount of conflict with respect to each other (if for no reason other than the existence of top management as an ultimate policeman), there will still be some possibility of disagreement and dissension.

Each of the transactions discussed above may go wrong in some way. When error occurs, the firm may suffer, and indeed may even go bankrupt. The purpose of the analysis presented here is to help managers avoid such errors. To indicate the use of the analysis, I will indicate briefly what sort of errors may occur in each of the listed transactions, and the chapters in the book which address each issue.

In order to avoid a hostile takeover, a group of senior managers of a firm undertakes a leveraged buyout. From the perspective of the owners of the firm, the stockholders, the error which may occur is that the managers may pay too little for the firm. Since the managers are in a better position than the stockholders to know the value of the firm, it will be difficult for the stockholders to be sure they are not being cheated. This issue is discussed in Chapter 5.

A firm must decide between issuing stock and borrowing in order to obtain $50 million in financing for a new project. If the wrong instrument is chosen the firm may pay too much for capital. On the other hand, it is also possible for the investment to be too risky. Different forms of finance create different incentives for efficient management and different risk structures, and the wrong choice may lead to less profits than are possible. This issue is addressed in Chapter 4.

One firm makes a hostile offer for another because the first thinks it can do a better job of managing the assets. Stockholders of both firms can lose if the decisions involved are not made correctly. If the buying firm pays too much, then its stockholders are losing. On the other hand, managers of the target firm may resist when its stockholders would benefit from the takeover. These issues are addressed in Chapter 5.

A defense contractor orders a customized machine which is absolutely essential for the successful completion of a contract. Since the machine is customized, there may be only one source. If the contractor deals incorrectly with this source, it may put itself in a position to be "held up." For example, the supplier may allege cost increases and raise its price when it is too late for the contractor to seek another source. This issue is addressed in Chapters 1 and 2.

A specialized consultant is needed to purchase and set up a firm's computer system, and a method of compensation must be devised. The purpose is to give the consultant proper incentives to buy the most cost-efficient system. Various methods of paying the consultant will effect his incentives. Perhaps it may even be more efficient to hire the consultant as a full-time employee. These issues are addressed in Chapter 3.

A successful fried chicken restaurant wants to sell franchises. It wants to structure its program so that its franchisees will provide the right amount of advertising and quality. From the point of view of the franchisor, the goal is to ensure that its franchisees will not degrade quality, because this will adversely effect all firms in the franchise, and thus the value of new franchises. Each franchisee also wants to be sure that the franchisor will police quality sufficiently so that its investment in the franchise will not become worthless. These issues are addressed in Chapter 7.

A high-quality firm in a business full of fly-by-night operators wants to be able to convince consumers of its quality. If it cannot convince consumers, then it cannot charge the premium needed to pay for the quality. On the other hand, consumers do not want to pay for high quality if they will not get it. The firm, thus, must be able to establish a reputation for excellence. This issue is addressed in Chapter 8.

A firm needs a steady supply of highly specialized machined parts, and must decide if it should make them or buy them. If it makes the parts, it will have difficulty in determining the correct cost. If it buys them, its supplier may be in a position to hold up the buyer who may be dependent on the seller. The make-or-buy decision is analyzed in Chapter 1, and, if a firm decides to buy, the buying decision is analyzed in Chapter 2.

The vice-president for marketing wants the vice-president for production to change the specifications on a product. This is a within-firm transaction, which is analyzed in Chapter 2.

A firm manufacturing a complex product, like a home computer, wants its distributors to demonstrate the use of the machine. If the manufacturing firm is not careful, some retailers will offer the product at a discount and will not provide any demonstration. Consumers will then go to full-service (and full-price) distributors for information, and buy the product from the discounter. Soon, the full-service firms will stop providing demonstrations as well. These issues are addressed in Chapter 6.

A purchasing agent places an order for five reams of standardized copying paper of a given size and quality with a local office supply store. This is a simple, not a complex, transaction. All the traders need to do is ensure that there is no fraud. These transactions are not the subject matter of this book.

There are certain general principles involved in complex transacting which are common to all of the cases mentioned, and to many other transactions. Since these principles transcend any one division of the business, it is useful for all managers to study them as a body. The purpose of this book is to set forth the principles of complex transacting. I do this both by giving some common examples and by stressing general principles which the manager can use to analyze any transaction.

As products and markets become increasingly complex, firms increasingly engage in more complex transactions. An expanding share of management time is spent on these transactions. Firms must reach agreement with other firms in many different circumstances. Some firms will supply inputs, which themselves will be increasingly complex with implications for quality control and monitoring. The firm will need to deal with other businesses which will buy its output or distribute its product. In all cases, the profitability and even the fate of the enterprise can rest on the intelligence with which these dealings are structured, and the wrong terms for a transaction can lead to bankruptcy or reorganization.

Moreover, in today's world, one class of transactions, "corporate control transactions," are increasingly common and increasingly vital. Even very large firms are subject to threats of hostile takeover, and the result of takeover is often the replacement of many managers, or the elimination of many managerial jobs. Leveraged buyouts and other recapitalization schemes are also increasingly common. These transactions are governed by the same principles as other transactions, and can be understood using the same tools.

In many cases, a firm will be able to select the type of players or firms with whom it transacts. The firm will often be in a position to determine whether to deal with an independent firm or to set up a subsidiary or division to perform some needed task. Therefore, before deciding the particulars of a complex transaction, a manager often must make a decision which will determine the nature of the players. The terms of a transaction with a subsidiary will be different than the terms with a franchisee, and these will, in turn, differ from the terms if the transaction should involve a separate, independent business. In this sense, principles of efficient transactions also determine the efficient organizational structure of the firm.

Added complications arise because organizational and transactional decisions are linked. It will be important to know what types of transactions can be efficiently executed in a given organizational structure before choosing that structure. In choosing between alternative organizational forms, it will be important to know how each will actually function if it is chosen. To determine this will require understanding the kinds of transactions each organizational form will do well. Before deciding whether to establish a franchise, for example, a manager will want to know just how she will ultimately deal with a franchisee if this method is chosen. The nature of the ultimate agreement between the firm and whatever type of distributor is chosen will itself help to determine the nature of the parties to the agreement. For example, if the operation is to be far away from the home base, then a franchise may facilitate control, while it will be easier to monitor a wholly owned subsidiary which is nearby.

The principles set forth here are not based on theoretical speculation, but on observation and study of the transactional behavior of successful firms. Scholars have spent time and effort in understanding the basis for observed conduct and in explaining why some behaviors work. Since the principles advanced here have generally been used by at least some firms, it may appear that they are known and that there is little purpose in writing or reading a book to explain them.* However, there are several reasons why this may not be so. Indeed, understanding the principles involved can benefit all managers, including even those who already apply them.

In some cases, managers may have fortuitously hit upon an efficient organization or transaction structure without fully understanding why it works. In some industries, there will be many firms with different organizational structures. One firm may have luckily chosen a structure which is more efficient than any other, and this firm will grow and thrive. Other firms, observing the growth, may copy the successful firm's methods. Nonetheless, none of the managers may understand why the methods work as well as they do. Managers of the original firm were lucky, and others have copied them. The first firm may itself have copied its procedures from another firm, perhaps in another industry.

For managers who are applying the principles successfully, this book will explain exactly why their organization is working well. This understanding may enable them to improve the structures by, for example, eliminating unneeded parts of the design. It may be that a structure with five parts is being used, when only one part is really needed for efficiency. Understanding why the arrangement works will then enable the manager to eliminate the unnecessary parts. After all, one arrangement may be better than any alternative actually used by others in the market (so that the firm using the design will thrive) and yet still not be the best possible. Understanding the structure will also enable managers to confidently extend the appropriate parts into other suitable areas. Market conditions may change, and it will be important to adapt to whatever new conditions come about. Those managers who

---

* Economists commonly take this view. The assumption is that behavior is optimal, and therefore economists can learn why firms behave as they do, but cannot improve on this behavior.

best understand the reasons for the success of existing arrangements will be in the best position to adapt to changes.

In other cases, some managers may have already figured out some of the principles discussed here. This book will help them systematize their knowledge and show them other parts of the organization where similar principles may be applied. Equally importantly, understanding the principles behind successful policies will enable managers to avoid errors committed when principles are wrongly applied.

Some readers lacking experience in successful management will be able to profit from this book by beginning their careers with additional knowledge. Experienced but as-yet-unsuccessful managers will be able systematically to learn skills which in others might seem intuitive and unlearned. By systematizing knowledge, we can teach that which seems to be the result of luck or intuition.

Over all, the principles set forth here will be useful to all managers. Owners of small businesses will be able to use them to make important structural decisions regarding the form of their firm. (For example, should the firm expand by direct investment or by franchising?) Managers in established enterprises will also be able to make use of these principles. (For example, how should a reputation for a new product be created, or how should labor agreements be structured?) The analysis will be helpful throughout the organization; some of the points (dealing with, for example, managerial compensation) will even be useful to the board of directors. Since some of these principles will make hostile takeovers less likely, understanding the ideas in this book may make jobs more secure. Moreover, in addition to the specific points made, once a reader understands the method of thinking and analysis used, he or she will be able to extend the results easily to new situations.

Before proceeding, a word about the basis of the principles discussed here is in order. This book has arisen out of a background in economics, and particularly those branches referred to as "law and economics," "industrial organization," and "transactions cost economics." (Some of the principles have been developed within the finance literature as well.) For some years, economists in these specialties have been studying the behavior of firms. In this study, many puzzling features of behavior surfaced. Old school economists often attributed any inexplicable behavior, such as exclusive transactions agreements, to a desire for monopoly. More recently, economists have come to realize that many of these previously puzzling features of transactions are grounded in good business practice and have no connection with any attempt to monopolize. In fact, they are essential to effective competition.

There is now enough known about such behavior to turn the intellectual process around. We have studied efficient firms and come to understand their behavior in terms of the business interests served by such behavior. Economists have used such understanding both to explain behavior and, on occasion, to defend behavior from overly militant antitrust authorities or private litigants. But the understanding can now be put to another use. We can now take the lessons learned from attempts to understand business behavior and instruct other firms in ways of increasing efficiency and profits. We can now systematically present principles for efficient management based on the study of those structures which have proven efficient for existing firms.

Study of the issues discussed in this book has often been done in conjunction with antitrust litigation. It has been alleged by the government or by private litigants that particular practices are anticompetitive, and economists have spent time and effort learning why firms have adopted certain practices. But it is important to realize that defendants in antitrust litigation are generally successful firms. Therefore, the principles examined have been those adopted by successful firms. Knowledge of these principles should help others to increase their own success.

There is a strong legal orientation in the literature explaining the behavior of firms. This has occurred for two reasons. First, one of the goals of the analysis was to study antitrust liability, and this occurs in a legal setting. Therefore, the analysis was aimed at understanding the business justification for observed behavior which could be presented during litigation.* Many of the concepts involved were legal rather than managerial or even economic concepts, and this imparted a legal flavor to the analysis. Some parts of the analysis have even been extended and applied within the legal literature.

Additionally, much of the analysis was of contractual relationships between firms at various levels. For example, many of the issues involve relationships between manufacturers and dealers. One of the important elements in managing transactions is the decision regarding use of

---

*An additional benefit of understanding the principles in this book may be stronger defenses in case of lawsuits. Some of the behaviors discussed here have been challenged in antitrust and other suits, and an ability to demonstrate that principles of efficiency were explicitly considered in adopting certain behaviors may facilitate a defense.

internal, firm-owned inputs versus hiring inputs on the market. Another important element is the structuring of contractual relations between the firm and its inputs, whether owned or hired. Therefore, many of the principles of transaction management will be instituted in contracts between the organization and its various clients. These clients include workers, customers, suppliers, and other firms which may, for example, distribute the product of the primary firm. Since these principles are expressed in contracts, they may appear to be legal concepts.

However, the real issues in drawing up these contracts are not legal. They are managerial. When a contract or transaction takes a certain form, the concern should not be with the legal form of the contract, but with the underlying business reality which makes that legal form desirable. This is a management concern, not a legal concern. The fact that a contract is a legal document should not confuse the issue. What is important is the business purpose of the contractual arrangement and of the underlying transaction.

A manager who understands the principles elucidated in this book will know what business purposes he wants a contract to fulfill. He will understand what duties to place on each party to an agreement, and what rewards should go to each. The manager will then be able to tell his lawyer what he wants to accomplish in the contracts, so that the lawyer will be able to draw up contracts which accomplish the goals of the managers.

In fact, even though this is not a law book in any sense, it may be as useful to corporate lawyers as to managers. For managers, the book will explain the business reality and the set of contracts and transactions which make business sense. For a lawyer, the book will help him understand what his business clients want to accomplish when they specify certain goals in their contracts. This is a different question than that dealt with in contract law. In normal contract law, one asks if a court will enforce a contract, and how it will be interpreted. Those are obviously important questions, and necessary considerations in drawing up contracts. But it is also important to make sure that the contract does what the manager wants it to do, and that is the goal of this book.

The book may help lawyers in another way. In practice and in reading cases, a business lawyer will see many types of contracts. It will be tempting and often helpful to a business client to transfer information from one contract to another. But it is important to understand why a particular contract was chosen in some circumstances and why it was successful. This book will provide this understanding.

Part I deals with the general acquisition of inputs by the firm. Chapter 1 considers a classic management problem, the make-or-buy decision. The analysis of this decision provides a useful introduction to the concepts used in the rest of the book. Chapter 2 continues the analysis by examining transactional terms when the make-or-buy decision leads to a "buy" but the purchased input is complex. Chapter 3 applies the analysis to labor markets.

Part II addresses issues associated with the capital structure of the firm. Chapter 4 provides a perspective on finance. Chapter 5 discusses restructurings and takeovers, an increasingly crucial part of business. Part III examines issues related to selling of products. Chapter 6 discusses relations between the firm and its distributors, and Chapter 7 considers the special case of franchising. Chapter 8 discusses the firm's reputation, and indicates ways of creating a good reputation. The book concludes with a summary.

Every day managers must make decisions regarding complex transactions. If a manager learns the principles set forth here and the ways of thinking which underlie these principles, he or she will be much more skilled at making these decisions; and the manager and the firm will prosper accordingly. If he does not learn these principles, either the firm will not do as well as it might, or it will do well under the management of someone else who does understand the principles.

BIBLIOGRAPHIC NOTE

I provide references at the end of each chapter. Some are citations of the technical literature in economics or the relevant legal literature. Others substantiate key points in the chapter. Fellow scholars should realize that I have not attempted to be comprehensive in my list of citations, and should not feel slighted. For example, wherever possible I have cited a survey article rather than the original source.

In addition, in the bibliography at the back of the book I list several basic, key sources for the material and for the form of analysis as well as a few general references that are cited throughout the book.

For their help in various ways, I would like to thank Henry Butler, Marsha Carow, Oliver Williamson, and Susan Woodward. I would also like to thank Glassman-Oliver Economic Consultants, my employer, for making resources available which enabled me to complete this book.

PART I

Inputs

$-1-$

Make or Buy?

The make-or-buy decision is a classic management concern. Every firm uses thousands of inputs, and for each there is a potential to either manufacture the input itself or acquire it on the market. In its broadest interpretation, this decision includes choices like hiring a consultant or employing internal labor to perform a given task. If a firm decides to make an input, it will transact internally with a division or another part of the firm. If it decides to buy, it will contract with another organization. In either case, it is important to understand the principles behind the structure chosen and behind the transaction. The make-or-buy decision is sometimes treated as an accounting or financial decision. While it is obviously important to perform accounting analyses and to choose the low-cost method, it is more important to understand the managerial basis of the decision.

One advantage of such understanding is that it will economize on decision-making time. There are virtually thousands of products that a firm will use, and each of them could potentially be produced internally. Managers need some method of deciding which products are good candidates for internal production and are worth a detailed internal cost analysis. Of course, some of the decisions are obvious—a messenger firm will not go through a complex analysis in order to decide whether or not to build its own cars. But other decisions are less obvious—if the messenger firm gets large enough, should it make its own uniforms or buy them? (Answer: Buy them.) The principles in this chapter will enable a manager to quickly and easily eliminate a whole host of products from consideration and analysis as potential products to make internally. (As seen below, the analysis of the messenger firm and its uniforms was an immediate consequence of the principles set forth in the remainder of this chapter.) This itself will save considerable managerial and accounting time.

The make-or-buy decision is often analyzed in terms of either capital market issues or technology. As indicated later, analysis of make-

or-buy choices cannot be done correctly if only technological or financial criteria are considered, although of course both are important to the decision. Rather, the correct analysis is a management analysis. The decision should depend on particular managerial elements, and the purpose of this chapter is to elucidate these elements.

USE OF THE MARKET

Subject to certain availability constraints, the firm wants to acquire inputs as cheaply as possible. When a competitive open market exists, this usually offers the most powerful method of controlling costs. If a product is made internally, then the firm must spend substantial managerial resources monitoring costs and efficiencies. In the market, on the other hand, simple shopping or seeking bids can easily and cheaply control costs. The best way to control costs is through the market. Provision of inputs by sellers facing competition provides powerful obvious incentives for low-cost, reliable production. Therefore, the first presumption should always be for purchasing inputs on the market. This conclusion should not be startling. After all, most firms buy most of their inputs, from office furniture to paper clips to automobiles to steel. It is only in special cases that the firm vertically integrates and makes its own inputs.

The analysis of the make-or-buy decision should therefore depend on examining factors which interfere with market provision of the inputs. Ultimately, these factors have to do with the cost and availability constraints mentioned above. However, the issue is not the existence of these constraints, but rather the reasons why the constraints may come into play. We must ask why the market will not provide the product cheaply, or why something may happen to make the input unavailable.

AVOID EXPLOITATION

The answer turns out to rest on the possibility that suppliers will be in a position to exploit the firm. This occurs when buying an input will subject the firm to a *holdup** problem which will potentially exist when the firm is subject to *opportunistic behavior.* When this happens, suppliers will be in a position to increase prices of inputs, or to demand

* Italicized terms are defined in the glossary.

additional payments before making needed inputs available in a timely manner.

Opportunistic behavior may occur when one firm can take advantage of its position with respect to another firm, as either a customer or a supplier. If a manager puts his firm in a position where someone can exploit it, the manager has laid the firm open to the risk of being the victim of opportunistic behavior. To avoid this, it is important to understand conditions under which this kind of behavior can occur.

The important point to keep in mind here is that there is a difference between the return needed on an investment before it is undertaken and the smaller return needed to maintain and operate an investment once it has been finished and the sunk costs are sunk. A manager will undertake an investment only if she can predict a return high enough to cover the firm's cost of capital. After the investment is undertaken it will often pay to continue to operate it at a rate of return which would not have been high enough to justify undertaking the investment in the first place. This difference—the difference between the amount which would be needed to justify an investment and the amount which justifies operating it after it is undertaken—is potentially available to be exploited from the firm. (Economists have given this quantity the particularly unpleasant name *quasirents.*) A good manager will be aware of the possibility of having quasirents exploited from his firm and will not place the firm in such a position for this to occur.

For an example which shows what is involved, consider a firm planning to get into the municipal garbage business.* There are two major parts of the business—inputs needed to pick up the refuse and a landfill for disposal. First, the firm has to consider the purchase of trucks and bid for a contract in a city. The current price for landfill capacity is $5 per ton and the firm plans to dispose of 1 million tons per year if it receives the contract. Trucks will cost $5 million (scrap value of $2.5 million) and the firm must invest $1 million in learning the local market and establishing contracts. Both the trucks and the goodwill of the initial investment will last fifteen years. Therefore, the amortized cost of this investment at 10 percent is about $800,000 per year. Drivers, maintenance, and other variable costs and the profit needed to make the endeavor worthwhile are $1.2 million per year. Therefore, for the 1

---

* This business was chosen partly because it shows that the principles developed here can be applied to even the most mundane activities. Moreover, firms in the trash business are increasingly finding it desirable to purchase landfills for just the reasons described here.

million tons involved, the firm must be able to charge at least $7 million ($5 million for landfilling, $1.2 million for variable costs, $800,000 return on fixed costs), or $7 per ton. (See Table 1.) If it cannot charge at least this amount, it will not bid on the contract.

But woe betide the manager who bids the job at $7 per ton and buys a fleet of trucks on the basis of these calculations. He has laid his firm open to severe exploitation by the owner of the landfill. The landfill owner can raise his price to $5.45 per ton and the truck operator will be better off paying it than shutting down. If he shuts down, he can sell the trucks for $2.5 million but he will still owe the rest of the cost of the trucks, another $2.5 million, plus the $1 million invested in establishing the business. If he sells the trucks and shuts down, he will still owe $460,000 per year to pay off the debt incurred in buying the trucks and setting up the business. If he continues to operate, he will lose $450,000 per year. In other words, the truck company loses $10,000 more by shutting down than by operating. Note, however, that the company would never have gone into the trash business if it had expected to pay $5.45. The $.45 per ton represents the quasirent which can be exploited from the company by the landfill operator behaving opportunistically.

TABLE 1: Holdup Possibility

Before Investment:

Capital cost of trucks .... $5 million
    Salvage value .... $2.5 million
Cost of establishing business .... $1 million

Annual fixed cost, 10% interest $800,000
Variable cost (gas, drivers) .... $1.2 million

Cost of landfilling, 1 million tons @ $5 per ton .... $5 million

Expected revenue required to bid .... $7 million
   ($7 per ton)

After Investment:

Fixed capital (assuming trucks are sold) .... $3.5 million

Annual fixed cost, 10 percent interest
   (equals annual loss if firm shuts down) $460,000

If landfilling rises to $5.45 per ton, the firm will lose $450,000 from operating. This is less than the $460,000 it will lose by shutting down. Therefore, the $460,000 represents the exploitable quasirent.

CONTRACTUAL SOLUTION?

A manager potentially facing this situation could try to draw up a contract in advance specifying the landfill price at $5.00 per ton. A sensible businessman would want such a contract, but it may not be enough. (In the next chapter, we discuss ways of structuring a transaction which will give the maximum protection when *vertical integration*—here a decision to buy the landfill—is not feasible.) A general principle is that all complex contracts are incomplete. It is impossible to specify a contract which will cover all eventualities.

First, of course, in times of inflation the landfill owner would not agree to a contract with a price fixed in money terms, so the contracting process becomes more complex. This issue, however, creates no particular difficulties. Prices may be tied to some general index, such as the Consumer Price Index, or to a narrower index of input prices. (In landfilling, it might be an index related to the minimum wage, the price of gasoline, and truck prices. This index will be more appropriate for this transaction than would be a general price index such as the Consumer or Producer Price Index, but since it will have to be designed and calculated specifically for this contract it will also be more expensive.)

The second, more substantial, difficulty is writing a contract with enough specificity to avoid any opportunistic behavior. While it may not appear so, landfilling is nonetheless a complex task. There are many ways in which the landfill can "hold up" the truck company for additional revenue. For example, it can make the trucks wait longer for their turn to dump their trash, thus increasing costs borne by the hauling company. It can also allow the company to use only relatively inaccessible parts of the landfill. It would be very difficult to specify the contract in enough detail to eliminate any possibility for exploitation. As environmental concerns regarding landfilling increase, and as liability for toxic waste disposal becomes more of a problem, holdup possibilities also increase.

This is not a legal problem. The difficulty is not that the lawyers are not clever enough to draw up a contract. If the businessman can tell them what types of opportunistic behavior might be involved, the lawyers can probably eliminate these behaviors by contract. The attorneys might even be able to suggest additional types of opportunistic behavior to avoid contractually—if they have seen other contracts or been party to litigation regarding such contracts or holdup situations.

But there remains a business problem. It is unlikely that a business-man can be clever enough to think up all the ways in which a landfill could exploit its position, and the lawyers will not have been exposed to contracts or litigation involving all forms of opportunism. Some events may be of such low probability that it does not pay to spend the resources to anticipate their occurrence, to decide what should happen if they occur, or to draft the rules which are appropriate for achieving these goals. (Most likely, more contracts in California than in Iowa specify the consequences of earthquake damage.) In certain situations, contracts will not be adequate to eliminate all possibilities of opportu-nism because they are incomplete in some way, and it may not be possible or worthwhile to make them complete.

Even if a contract could be written with sufficient specificity, en-forcement would be difficult. In many of the cases where exploitation is possible, time is important, so that the delay associated with litigation over a contract breach might itself impose substantial costs on the firm. In the garbage example, landfills by definition fill up, so that by the time the truck company might win a suit, there may be no space left for dumping. Whatever damages can be collected may not be adequate to compensate for the lost quasirents.

VERTICAL INTEGRATION

What is the solution? As the story is told, the best solution is for the truck company to buy the landfill before bidding the hauling contract. (Actually, an option on the landfill contingent on getting the municipal hauling business would probably be the chosen method.) If the same company owns the landfill and the trucks, there is no possibility for exploitation of the quasirents. This is a case where the firm should clearly consider seriously "making," not "buying." Ownership, what economists call *vertical integration,* is the answer.* The landfill and the trucking company are worth more under joint ownership than they are worth if owned separately.

What features of this example make ownership compelling? The answer is the close relationship between the capital needed for trash hauling and the capital needed for landfilling. Once the city contract is awarded, the hauling business is dependent upon the landfill. The landfill is a *specific asset* for the hauling business. The two sets of assets

---

*Actually, this also depends on the costs of such integration, discussed below.

are closely linked, and therefore a possibility for opportunistic behavior exists if they are separately owned.

This dependence, however, may be symmetric. It is quite possible that the hauling company will be able to hold up the landfill. This is particularly true if the hauling company is one of the major users, or the sole user, of the landfill. Just as the landfill is a specific asset for the truck company, the trucking business is a specific asset for the landfill. The hauling company can perhaps offer too low a payment to the landfill, threatening to use another landfill further away, and exploit some of the quasirent invested by the landfill owner.

The key point is not that vertical integration will save haggling costs; it is much more fundamental. If holdup possibilities exist, then efficient transactions may not occur. Socially and privately desirable investments may not be undertaken, and some efficient deals will not be done.

The possibility of holdup will deter the landfill owner as well as the truck company from undertaking otherwise desirable investments. For example, if the truck company asks the landfill to undertake some additional investment, such as building new access roads, the landfill owner will hesitate because this will then give the truck company a holdup possibility over the landfill. After the road is built, there are quasirents associated with it, and these can be exploited by the truck company just as easily as the quasirents on the truck business can be exploited by the landfill. The trucks are a specific asset for the landfill, just as the landfill is a specific asset for the trucks.

If the landfill and the truck company are owned by the same party, only then will neither party be subject to holdup. Common ownership will eliminate the possibility of opportunistic behavior being used to exploit quasirents. Moreover, it does not really matter who buys whom. The landfill owner could just as easily own the truck company as the other way around. The only important point is that both inputs be under common ownership. When the two assets are under joint ownership, all efficient investments will be undertaken. When they are not, some efficient deals will not be done. Some economists would even say that separate ownership can lead to market failure.

The two assets together are worth more if they are owned by one party than if they are separately owned, and this is the fundamental requirement for vertical integration. It also means that efficient ownership structures should be observed in the market. The hauling company can pay more for the landfill than anyone else because of this increased value of joint ownership.

It is the combination of exploitable quasirents (which is a common business phenomenon) and someone in a position to exploit them (a less common event, and one to be avoided) which should lead to such vertical integration. It is only when both features are present that vertical integration is useful. For instance, it would not pay the hauling company to buy a truck factory because there is no "asset specificity" between a truck manufacturer and a hauling firm. There are many competitive bidders for contracts to sell trucks, and if one truck company tried to hold up the hauling company, the latter could easily turn to another. (Since there are many clothing manufacturers in a position to make uniforms to any desired specification with no delay, there is no holdup possibility, which is why the messenger firm discussed above need not vertically integrate into uniform manufacture.)

Note that the form of business organization chosen will also effect the type of assets used. We may think of alternative production processes. One involves specific assets and is more productive; the other uses only general, nonspecialized assets but is less productive. (A more productive process involving general assets would dominate, and so need not be considered since if it is available it will always be chosen.) Then which process is chosen will depend in part on the structure to be used. If there is to be vertical integration, then it becomes efficient to invest in more specific assets and use the more efficient process. Thus, there is an interrelationship between type of capital used and the organizational structure of the firm, and a manager should realize that both decisions should be made simultaneously.

NOT MONOPOLY

The possibility of being held up is not the same as being a victim of a monopolist. A monopoly position is not required for quasirent exploitation. Before the truck company bids on the hauling contract, there are many potential bidders. None has any monopoly power. Nonetheless, after a bid is successful, the bilateral monopoly position between the hauling company and the landfill exists. What was a competitive position before actual investment now becomes a noncompetitive position, precisely because the investment creates exploitable quasirents. This switch—from a competitive position before investment in undertaken to a bilateral monopoly after the investment—is sometimes called the *fundamental transformation.*

Consider a situation in which there is only one landfill but many hauling companies. The landfill will charge a high, monopoly price to all hauling companies. Hauling companies will make their plans and undertake investments on the basis of this high price. But the monopolist landfill will not raise the price after the hauling company has undertaken its investment in order to exploit the quasirents. If the landfill did this, then future entrants into hauling would quickly learn of this behavior and refrain from entering, reducing demand for the services of the landfill. A monopoly position will lead to high prices, but it takes more than this to generate exploitable quasirents and thus the incentive for vertical integration.

It is inappropriate to use the antitrust laws in situations of asset specificity, even though these situations are characterized by bilateral monopoly after contracting and investing in specific assets has occurred. The antitrust laws are aimed at protecting consumers from high prices and reduced quantities caused by exploitation of a monopoly position. However, the appropriation of quasirents does not lead to a price increase to consumers. There are transfers between firms, but they do not effect market prices since quasirents, being returns on sunk investments, do not effect prices.

Moreover, the main difference in this context between antitrust and contract law is that antitrust has multiplied (trebled) damages. The theory behind such damages is that some violations will not be detected, so that penalties must be greater to provide sufficient deterrence. However, contractual opportunism occurs in situations where there are two well-defined parties dealing with each other. Therefore, such opportunism would be detected with a very high probability, so that there would be no benefit from multiplied damage payments. There might well be some costs in terms of overdeterrence, since multiplied damage payments might cause some firms to maintain contracts even when it would be more efficient to break them. For these reasons, it is appropriate to treat situations involving exploitable quasirents under contract law, but not under antitrust law.*

CHANGING CIRCUMSTANCES

Where there are specific assets, changes in circumstances may lead to changes in efficient modes of cooperation and gains from coopera-

---

* The only benefit from using the antitrust laws is that litigation under this body of law commonly relies on economists as experts in the efficiency of particular arrangements. This is less common as yet in contract law, so that the courts may be less likely to understand the efficiency justifications for particular arrangements.

tion may increase or decrease. When there is no integration, and assets are separately owned, owners of assets will then bargain over responses to changed circumstances and over the division of gains or losses from these same circumstances. Such bargaining is costly and time consuming. While the parties are bargaining, they are not acting, and therefore money is being lost. An additional benefit of organization within a firm is the power of the owner or manager to order terms of transactions when the best set of terms changes, and therefore avoid this loss from bargaining. The right to control the use of assets within a firm is sometimes called the *residual decision right*. In situations where change is likely or where delays from bargaining are costly, organization within a firm is more desirable.

ASSET SPECIFICITY

In the example of the landfill and the hauling company, the relation between the two assets takes the form it does because of a geographic linkage between the two assets. This is a common form of asset specificity. Another example of site-created specificity would be the relationship between a coal-burning electrical generation plant located at the mouth of a coal mine and the mine itself. We would expect common ownership. Similarly, Alcoa aluminum bought many bauxite mines because it often paid to build smelters at the site of the mine, presenting obvious holdup problems if mines and smelters were owned by different parties. Common ownership of steel production and steel milling can be explained in the same way. It is desirable to have steel milling located near steel production because of the savings in reheating costs, but this common siting could create holdup problems without common ownership.

But geographic linkage is not the only form that asset specificity can take. Another example is physical asset specificity. An investment may be undertaken in a product which is useful to only one customer. The traditional example is the early relation between General Motors and Fisher Body. Originally, GM contracted with Fisher for auto bodies. But Fisher realized that it would be subject to a holdup problem once it build a plant to make bodies for GM as the car maker would then be in a position to exploit the quasirents associated with the plant. Therefore, Fisher contractually required GM to buy *all* of its bodies from Fisher, thus removing GM's potential holdup power. But this, on the other hand, created power for Fisher to hold up GM. GM tried to protect itself contractually by fixing prices and other terms of the transaction. Demand for bodies grew faster than anticipated, leading to lower costs for Fisher, and Fisher's profits were greater than GM had anticipated. GM was unhappy with a situation giving Fisher excess profits based on an erroneous market forecast. Ultimately, GM and Fisher merged.

INFORMATION PROBLEMS

A seller may exploit a buyer by selling a lower quality product than was expected or agreed upon. This will increase the profits of the seller at the expense of the buyer. The seller can know more about quality than can the buyer, which is an example of *asymmetric information,* a general problem which occurs frequently. Vertical integration can eliminate this incentive to exploit. The general point is this: The more difficult it is to measure quality of an intermediate good, the more likely it is for vertical integration to be justified. Additionally, ownership of goods should change hands at that point in the production process where quality monitoring and measurement is least costly.

In deciding whether to make or buy an input, these principles are relevant and should be considered by a manager. He should be more willing to buy, rather than make, a good whose quality is easy to measure. Additionally, where there is an option, a manager should structure the purchase decision so that he is buying at a point where measurement is relatively easy. For example, a firm which needs dyed cotton cloth for an input may find it most efficient to buy greige goods (undyed cotton cloth) and perform the dying itself because costs of measuring quality of undyed material should be lower than costs of measuring quality of dyed material.

ALTERNATIVE STRATEGIES

While the presence of exploitable quasirents is necessary for vertical integration to be worthwhile, it is not sufficient. The presence of potential holdup problems does not by itself guarantee that such integration will be beneficial. Vertical integration reduces possibilities for cost control as compared with use of markets, so the cost of the holdup problems must be greater than the loss in efficient cost savings for such integration to pay.

Returning to our original example, if it would cost the hauling company $.50 per ton more than the landfill company to operate the landfill, then vertical integration would not pay. If the hauling company wanted to buy the landfill, it would have to pay a price for the landfill based on current conditions, assuming the lowest cost of running the landfill. If the hauling company would be less efficient than the current operator in running the landfill, then it would suffer a loss on its purchase. If this loss were more than the exploitable quasirent (calculated at $.40 per ton), then it would be cheaper to be exploited than to buy the landfill. The landfill would undertake a similar analysis of its costs of running the hauling company.

It is at this point that the traditional make-or-buy analysis begins. The traditional accounting or cost analysis assumes the data which has been discussed. That is, this accounting analysis examines the lowest cost alternative for a given set of costs for each action. But the interesting managerial questions are those related to the data inputs into the accounting process. Unless the correct structure is placed on the problem, including the correct measures for costs of being victimized by opportunistic behavior, the answer from the accountant will be wrong.

When there are specific assets and exploitable quasirents but it does not pay to make the product internally, a difficult problem arises for the firm. In these circumstances it becomes important to protect oneself from exploitation. There are many contractual methods of providing such protection, which will be discussed in the next chapter.

OTHER EXPLANATIONS

Vertical integration is sometimes explained by technological factors. The example above of steel milling and steel production is often cited as a technological explanation for common ownership. It is said that both operations must be under such ownership because the technology requires it.

There are true benefits from having steel production and milling in one location. These are technological, and are based on the savings in reheating costs associated with rolling steel when it is still hot. But a technological linkage by itself does not require vertical integration and common ownership. Technology does not dictate ownership. For example, it is quite possible to think of a steel mill buying hot steel ingots from a furnace located in the same building through an arm's-length transaction, with no common ownership. There is a well-defined market price for steel of a certain grade, and one can easily think of a contract specifying a mechanism for determining the transaction price based on market prices, with the savings from avoiding extra reheating split between the parties.

But no steel mill would put itself in the position of being dependent on a single furnace for its supply of steel. No furnace would put itself in the position of being forced to sell all of its output to a single mill. Common ownership is required by the transaction structure of the deal, not by the technology.

It is sometimes argued that vertical integration is justified because a firm needs a secure source of supply and can only establish such a secure source by integrating. For example as a professor, writer, and consultant, I cannot function without a secure source of paper clips, paper and ink for my printer. Nonetheless, I do not find it worthwhile buying paper mills, paper clip factories, and ink manufacturers. I do not worry about a secure source of supply because these items are readily available on the market.

When would someone worry? Only if the supplier is in a position to hold up the buyer. If a small office supply store in an isolated town induced me to move there by promising a secure source of paper and other supplies, I might be subject to a holdup problem after I had moved. The quasirents which could be exploited would be the costs of moving. In this case, I might want to use some method (although obviously not vertical integration) to guarantee my supplies. But in the normal course, where no holdup possibility exists, vertical integration is not needed to guarantee security. It should not be surprising that those cases where vertical integration is justified on the basis of securing supplies are cases where asset specificity and other conditions for potential holdup prevail.

Some argue that firms must sometimes buy inputs because they lack the capital needed to acquire facilities for internal production. It is very unlikely that this will be the case if the cost analysis is done correctly. When holdup problems occur, this means that the aggregate value of both firms under common ownership is greater than their value under separate ownership. A correctly performed accounting analysis will demonstrate this. This analysis should be a powerful tool to bring to the capital markets. The landfill is worth $3.5 million (the present value at 10 percent of $460,000 per year) more to the trucking company than it is worth to the current owner. If the current value of the landfill is $40 million, then its value to the truck company is $43.5 million, a substantial increment. The hauling company can pay a premium over the landfill's current value and still come out ahead, and it is difficult to imagine that there is no lender who would be willing to finance such a profitable transaction.

WHO SHOULD OWN AN ASSET?

So far, we have focused on the decision as to the location of an activity: Should an input be produced within a firm or produced outside and bought by the firm? A related issue is the ownership of an asset: Should the firm own some asset or should the asset be owned by another firm? This decision is related to the production decision since assets are used in productive activities, but some additional insights can be gained by focusing separately on the asset ownership issue. The specific question is this: Assets A (owned by Firm A) and Assets B (owned by Firm B) are jointly used in production. There are three options: Firm A can own A and B; Firm B can own A and B; or Firm A can own A and firm B can own B. That is, there are two possibilities for integration (A owns everything, or B does) and one option of nonintegration.

But, first, what is meant by ownership in functional, not legal, terms? Associated with any asset will be a set of rights, and thus ownership is defined as the possession of *residual rights,* where residual rights are those which are not specified in the contract. In general, the advantage of ownership is the ability to prevent opportunistic behavior associated with the use of the asset with respect to residual (noncontractual) rights, as discussed above. However, it is possible to specify in more detail the nature of the solution to this problem.

In particular, the assets should be owned by that party whose investments in the asset are more important for maximizing total productivity. If this is true of neither party, then the firms should remain nonintegrated. The value of using this approach to decision making is that it forces us to look at investment possibilities in deciding on the location of ownership. An example will make the usefulness clear.

The asset whose ownership is examined here is a client list in the insurance industry. It is possible for either the agent who sells the insurance to own the list (so that the agent has the right to sell the customers a different brand of insurance) or for the company to own the list (so that the company retains the customer even if, for example, the agent leaves the company). The efforts of both agents and companies jointly determine the extent to which customers will remain with the company. For example, agents can do a good job of tailoring policies to customers, or they can do a good job of selecting customers who are likely to remain. If agents own the list, they can also switch the customer to another policy. Companies can change the terms of insurance so that some customers leave if, for example, the company decides that certain areas are too expensive to insure.

In order to provide agents with proper incentives to undertake those investments which are under the control of the agent for retaining customers, commissions must depend partly on the initial payment of the customer and partly on the customer's continuing payments; this feature of commission does not depend on the ownership of the list. Companies get the residual share of the ongoing commission structure, so that they also have incentives to try to maintain clients. Once a policy is written, there are actions which either party can take to reduce the chances of renewal. If the agent does not do enough to retain the customer, then the company loses, and conversely. Therefore, both parties can lose from the behavior of the other. We want to structure ownership so as to minimize the costs associated with *shirking* by either party.

Ownership of the list should be with the agent in those circumstances where loss of the customer is most sensitive to the agent's actions. As the influence of the agent falls, ownership should shift to the company. If we consider different types of insurance, we find exactly this pattern. "Whole life" insurance is the type in which renewal is most likely (because annual lifetime premium payments depend on the age at which the policy is first purchased, so that switching companies is expensive) and in the case of whole life most client lists are owned by companies. Next might be "term life," where renewal is less likely than in whole life because premiums are generally fixed for a five-year, rather than lifetime, period. Property and casualty insurance are the types where switching is most likely because premiums are fixed for only one year. As the theory predicts, more client lists are owned by companies in the case of term than in the case of casualty, and most in whole life.

In sum, the theory of asset ownership involves structuring ownership in such a way as to promote efficient investment in assets. In general, an asset should be owned by that party who can most efficiently invest in the asset. This principle has been followed in the insurance industry with respect to ownership of client lists. In the next chapter, the same principles will be applied to decisions regarding the hiring of internal labor or outside contractors for some tasks.

BUYING OR SELLING A BUSINESS

If a decision is made to vertically integrate, then the firm will often buy an existing, ongoing business. In this section, such an acquisition is discussed from the transactional point of view, which is useful in its own right because such transactions are themselves important. In addition, it indicates some of the transactional issues associated with a major purchase, and introduces some concepts which will prove useful later. In particular, possibilities of opportunism in the transaction, and ways of protecting against opportunism are discussed. The analysis is structured so that it will be useful either to the firm (B) buying a business or to the firm (S) selling.

In a transaction for the sale of a business (or indeed, in any transaction) there are two separate issues. First, Should the transaction occur; and, second, if so, At what price? Assume, for example, that a business is worth $15 million to the buyer and $10 million to the seller, perhaps for reasons discussed above, such as the reduction in opportunism which will be brought about through common ownership. Then there is room for a transaction, and value to both parties can be increased by undertaking the transaction. There is a surplus of $5 million to be divided between the parties. However, the transaction can occur at any price between $10 and $15 million, and both parties have an interest in the price. The seller of course wants as high a price as possible, and the buyer as low as possible. There is room for disagreement over splitting of the $5 million surplus between the parties. The parties will negotiate over the price, and much bargaining will be involved.

For the most part, in this book issues related to bargaining are neglected, assuming that the parties have agreed on a price. The book does discuss, however, ways in which each can avoid being the victim of opportunism (which would lead to a different price being paid, since opportunism adds to costs). In a complex transaction such as one involving the sale of a business, this is not a simple matter.

The issues discussed here are generally handled in the contracts for the sale of the business. Responses to these issues are drafted by the attorneys representing the parties. However, in this context the attorneys are acting as "transactions engineers" rather than as attorneys. The issues are transactional, and the important matters could be decided upon by others, although at some level an attorney would need to draft the agreement. Nonetheless, as a manager, it is important to understand the managerial issues behind the legal language. Such an understanding will be useful both to help the attorney in achieving the party's goals in writing the contract and in interpreting any contract which the attorney may present. It is also useful for attorneys to have an explicit understanding of the business basis for the terms of the contract.

Time-Related Issues

In many cases, the transaction will not take place instantaneously. Rather, there may be an agreement that B will buy the business, with closing at some future point in time. Moreover, the value at the time of closing may depend on events which occur between the time of the agreement and the time of closing. In this case, it will be useful to agree on a method of valuation which will not create any inefficient incentives. For one example, the value of the business at closing may depend on profits earned during the interim period. If the parties cannot agree on the expected level of profits during this period, a contract which makes the transaction price at the time of closing a function of actual profits in the interim will be useful. (Note that this is not a disagreement over splitting of the surplus from the transaction: Both parties agree about the value of sales. The disagreement is over what will actually occur in the future.) A possible agreement, for example, would be that the transaction price will increase by 75 percent of the amount of profits over the relevant period.

This will not be a complete response, however, because it also creates inefficient incentives. For example, the selling party might have incentives to underspend on maintenance during the interim period. This underspending would increase earnings, although it would reduce the value of the company by more than this increase (which is why it is inefficient). Nonetheless, since S has an interest in earnings only until the time of closing, such actions would be in his interest.

To solve problems of this sort, complex contractual terms including contingent payments based on profits or other measures of future performance (called "earnouts") are used. These terms are aimed both at controlling incentives of the sort discussed above and also at specifying reactions to various possible changes which might occur in the world during the interim period. For example, to solve the maintenance problem the contract might specify that a certain amount would be spent on maintenance, or it might have the buyer pay for maintenance. A substantial part of the drafting of contracts will deal with these issues. However, it is important for management to understand what is involved because the attorneys doing the drafting may not have the deep business understanding necessary to correctly specify incentives for this particular business and may not know as much as management about potential forms of opportunism in this industry.

Informational Issues

A second set of issues in the sale of a business have to do with information. Considerable information is already possessed by the seller, since he has been running the business, and the contract should devise methods of transferring this information to the buyer. Additionally, it will sometimes be useful to produce new information which neither party possesses, and the contract should facilitate production of this information at the lowest possible cost. Finally, the agreement will provide for efficient verification of the information.

Since the seller has been operating the business, he clearly knows more about many issues than does the buyer. It is in the interests of both parties for the seller to give the buyer access to whatever information the buyer wants. If the buyer requests a piece of information and the seller refuses, the buyer will assume that the information is completely adverse, and will devalue his offer accordingly. If the buyer must spend resources developing information which the seller could transmit more cheaply, then the buyer will correspondingly reduce the amount he is willing to pay for the business. Thus, it is in the seller's interest to make information acquisition by the buyer as cheap as possible.

In some cases, there may be valuable information which is unknown to either party. For example, neither party may know in detail the interrelationships between the buyer's and seller's business, since this information was not valuable before a transaction was planned. This information can probably be provided most cheaply by the buyer, although with inputs from the seller. Other information may deal with issues which only arise in the context of the transaction, such as the effect of the acquisition on contracts with third parties. This may most cheaply be provided by the counsel for the seller.

And, of course, information is valuable only to the extent that it is true. Parties may have incentives to provide false information if this enables them to get more of the surplus from the transaction. Therefore, it is important to create devices which enable the parties (and particularly the buyer) to verify the information provided. There are two common methods for verification of information: indemnification and third-party certification.

Indemnification is an agreement by the seller to compensate the buyer if any information provided by the seller turns out to be false. (This may be viewed as a *hostage* or *bond* provided by the seller, concepts discussed in more detail in the next chapter.) Such terms are most commonly provided by sellers of private companies. Sellers of public companies have other ways of guaranteeing true information. For example, the management of a public company may expect to remain with the new buyer, and such post-sale contracts can themselves serve as hostages. (If the manager lies to the buyer, then when the buyer finds out, he will fire the manager.) The top managers of private companies are generally the owners, and the transaction itself will normally represents too large a fraction of the wealth of the owner for such post-employment agreements to serve as a hostage, so that explicit agreements may be necessary. Public companies must also disclose a good deal of information to the Securities and Exchange Commission, and must have this information audited, so that it is more difficult for such companies to misrepresent themselves, and therefore less value from indemnification.

A second method of verification is to rely on third parties for certifying the validity of information. These third parties may be independent lawyers retained by the parties, investment bankers, or accounting firms. In all cases, these third parties have valuable reputations; indeed, the value of the reputation of a major law firm or investment banking firm may be greater than the value of the particular business being sold. Therefore, reliance on such third parties may be a convincing method of certifying information. Of course, the third parties, knowing that their reputations are at risk, will themselves spend substantial amounts on verifying information before they attest to its truth. Indeed, the large fees charged by these firms in many transactions may be reflections of the potential loss of their reputations if they make errors.

SUMMARY

In general, the initial presumption should be for outside purchase of needed inputs, rather than internal production. Internal production is worthwhile only under a specialized set of circumstances. These conditions ultimately boil down to the existence of exploitable quasi-rents which would be associated with outside purchase. These require that there be assets specific to one firm under the ownership of another firm. The existence of such specific assets means that there may be exploitable quasirents, and that it is worth considering the possibility of vertical integration.

Internal production also becomes more desirable if there are costs of measuring quality of inputs. Rights to control decisions are also important in circumstances where there are specialized assets and possibilities of changed circumstances. If there are no specialized assets and no measurement costs, the firm should not even contemplate internal production. Other explanations, such as technological reasons or capital cost arguments, cannot give correct answers to the vertical integration question. The ultimate answer is managerial, and depends on the factors enumerated above. In examining the issue of ownership of assets, it was determined that assets should be owned by those parties whose investment are most important in increasing the value of the asset.

If the firm decides on vertical integration, then it may be useful to acquire an ongoing company. There are important issues involved in establishing the terms for such transactions, which have to do with timing of the transaction and production and verification of information related to the transaction. In all cases, there are possibilities for opportunism, and parties should protect themselves from such behavior.

REFERENCES

Blair, Roger D. and Kaserman, David L. *Antitrust Economics,* Chapters 11–12. Homewood, Ill.: Richard D. Irwin, 1985.

Coase, Ronald. "The Nature of the Firm." *Economica* 4 (1937):386. Reprinted in *The Economic Nature of the Firm: A Reader,* edited by Louis Putterman. New York: Cambridge University Press, 1986.

Gilson, Ronald J. "Value Creation by Business Lawyers: Legal Skills and Asset Pricing." *Yale Law Journal* 94 (1984):239.

Goldberg, Victor. "Regulation and Administered Contracts." *Bell Journal of Economics* 7 (1976):426.

Grossman, Sanford J., and Hart, Oliver D. "The Costs and Benefits of Ownership: A Theory of Vertical and Lateral Integration." *Journal of Political Economy* 94 (1986):691.

Holmstrom, Bengt R., and Tirole, Jean. "The Theory of the Firm." In *Handbook of Industrial Organization,* Richard Schmalensee and Robert Willig. New York: North Holland, 1989.

Klein, Benjamin, Crawford, Robert, and Alchian, Armen. "Vertical Integration, Appropriable Rents, and the Competitive Contracting Process." *Journal of Law and Economics* 21 (1978):297. Reprinted in *The Economic Nature of the Firm,* edited by Louis Putterman.

Williamson, Oliver. *The Economic Institutions of Capitalism,* Chapters 4–5. New York: Free Press, 1985.

— 2 —

Buying Complex Products

In the last chapter, we discussed the make-or-buy decision—one that should arise only if there are specific assets involved in a product. If not, the firm should buy the input, and need not perform any significant analysis. A firm may decide to make an input because a decision to buy would leave it subject to holdup or exploitation by its suppliers. In some circumstances, existence of specific assets will create appropriable quasirents, and a firm may produce an input to avoid being the victim of such appropriation.

However, there are costs to internal production as well as benefits. First, the firm may not use enough of an input to achieve all potential economies of production associated with this product. These economies may be of two types: *economies of scale* or *economies of scope.* Economies of scale exist when costs of production fall as more of a particular product is produced. Economies of scope occur when costs fall as more different types of products are produced. Even though some product is specialized for a firm, it may be produced in a facility producing enough similar products to obtain such economies. For instance, if a specialized part is made in a machine shop, the part is specialized and a firm which needs the part may be subject to holdup problems. Nonetheless, a machine shop can clearly produce the part cheaper than a firm which merely uses the part as an input because the machine shop produces many similar products and the same labor and equipment can be used. If a firm should decide to set up a machine shop for internal production of only the needed specialized part, it loses the benefits of these cost savings. If it sets up a machine shop for production of the needed input and plans to operate the shop for the market, then it is in the machine shop business, a business for which it may not be qualified and in which it may have high costs.

23

Second, internal production leads to the loss of the benefits of discipline imposed by the market. Market incentives for efficiency and low-cost production are the most powerful incentives available. Internal production requires that the firm forego these benefits. The firm must instead rely on internal monitoring to control costs. Therefore, it will sometimes be desirable to buy an input on the market, even if this will subject the firm to the sort of expropriation associated with specific assets and appropriable quasirents. When it does pay to buy specialized inputs, however the firm should take care to protect itself as much as possible from opportunistic behavior by suppliers.

The analyses in this and in the previous chapter are related in an additional way. The results of the make-or-buy decision depend on the expected terms under which the firm will buy the input. If the firm decides to buy rather than to make some input, then it will engage in the kinds of transactions discussed in this chapter. Therefore, before deciding whether to make or buy some input, the firm should consider what types of arrangements it will use to protect itself if it should decide to use the market. It is also important to understand the kinds of contracts and the costs of contracting if the decision is to buy. If it will be difficult to devise an efficient mechanism for buying some input, then a firm may decide to make it, even though this also has costs.

EFFICIENT CONTRACTS

One party to a contract, the "performing party," agrees to undertake some task; the other party, the "paying party," agrees to pay for this task. In many transactions, either party may be in a position to breach. The performing party may not perform as agreed upon. Products may be below standards in quality, or delivery may be late. The paying party may not pay the full amount, or may delay payment. Either participant may be in a position to behave opportunistically, although there are more opportunities for shirking by the performing party since court enforcement of a simple money payment will be straightforward.

Moreover, when the contract is being negotiated and written, both parties generally have an incentive for the contract to be efficiently written, monitored, and enforced. The performing party will be able to charge a higher price than otherwise if he can, in some way, guarantee his performance, and he wants to be sure of being paid. The paying party will be able to pay a lower price if he can guarantee that collection will not be a problem, and of course the buyer wants to be sure of the quality of the product.

As a result, both parties to a transaction have an incentive to devise efficient enforcement mechanisms. If we observe, for example, that a contract imposes heavy penalties for nonperformance, this does not mean that the paying party is in control and has forced the performing party to accept unfavorable terms, or that there is unequal bargaining power. It may well be that the performing party suggested these terms knowing that he could charge a higher price if he could credibly commit himself to execute the agreement.

An exception would occur if one party negotiates with the intention of breaching its agreement and behaving opportunistically. Such bad faith bargaining is an extreme example of opportunism, and may rise to the level of fraud. In this case, the party planning a breach would not want an efficient contract. It is obviously important not to contract with parties planning breach. One way to avoid dealing with such parties is to rely on reputation.

Another way to protect against such intentions is to propose methods of efficient contracting; if the other party rejects these proposals, this may be a sign that he or she is not negotiating in good faith. In fact, this method is more general. There are several situations in which we can, in part, measure the intentions or expectations of parties with whom we are contemplating transacting by offering certain contractual terms and observing if parties accept the terms. In this case, we are using transaction terms as a method of getting our partners to *self-select* with respect to some aspect of interest.

In reading this chapter, there are two things a manager should look for. First, he should look for ways to commit his trading partners to maintain their agreements. This is important because it will reduce the chances of his firm suffering from the potential opportunistic behavior of its partner. But a manager should also look for ways to commit his own firm to fulfill its agreements. If a manager can so commit his firm and inform his trading partners of this, such commitments will improve the terms on which he transacts. Naturally, at all times, both parties can gain from efficient contracts and agreements.

ARE THE COURTS ENOUGH?

Only as a last resort should a manager rely on an explicit contract enforced by a court of law to protect the firm's interest in a transaction.

There are several reasons why it is not good policy to rely on courts and contracts where other alternatives are available.

First, it is impossible to write a contract which is sufficiently complete to protect a firm's interests in a situation of complex contracting. Even ignoring opportunism, there are too many unforeseen and unforeseeable events which might make compliance with a contract impossible. This is particularly true of the sort of contracts at issue here. Typically, the relevant contracts will be long term and will deal with complex issues. As more and more eventualities are covered, costs of drafting and interpreting a contract will increase, so there are limits to the list of occurrences which it is worthwhile to include in a contract. Even if managers seek to write a comprehensive contract, this will not be possible.

Since the contracts are long term, conditions can change in unpredictable ways. For example, the major inflation of the 1960s and 1970s caught many people off guard, and many firms suffered substantial losses as a result. (The origins of the problems in the savings and loan industry were due to these losses.) In contracts, prices are relatively easy to control for, and presumably now people would be less likely to write a fixed-price contract without some inflation adjustment involved; where such contracts are written, the paying party will need to pay a premium, as in acquiring a fixed rate rather than an adjustable mortgage. (People might be less prone to contractually adjust for deflation, since we have not seen a deflationary period since the 1930s.) Nonetheless, since many contracts were written in terms which did not control such a simple matter as price-level changes, there are clearly many more subtle changes which may occur and which are not specified in all contracts.

Similar problems arise because of the complex nature of the contracts and the uncertainties which such complexity engenders. For example, in the original contract between GM and Fisher Body, discussed in the last chapter, neither party anticipated the rapid growth in demand for metal-closed auto bodies relative to open-wood bodies. This rapid growth meant that Fisher's costs of production were much lower and its profits much higher than GM had anticipated, and it was this change in costs and profits which caused the parties to renegotiate and ultimately merge.

Third, in addition to the long-term nature of the contracts and the complexity involved, there is also the possibility of opportunism. Opportunistic firms will look for ways to cheat on a contract, and clever firms will be able to find ways, no matter how intelligently the contract is drafted. There are specific mechanisms available to avoid or reduce the possibility of being the victim of opportunism, and these mechanisms should be used wherever possible, whether or not there is an explicit contract.

Finally, there are many provisions which parties might like to put in contracts but which the courts will not enforce. For example, sometimes parties would like to specify the amount of damages in the event of breach. If courts determine that the specified amount is really a measure of actual damages (called *liquidated damages* in law), they will enforce the contract, but if they determine that the specified amount is too large, they will call it *punitive* and refuse enforcement. Of course, once breach has occurred, an opportunistic breacher will have an incentive to allege that damages are punitive, and litigation might follow. The point is, however, that it is not always possible to write an explicit, enforceable contract to achieve a given goal.

If a contract is written, what should be the term? There are advantages and disadvantages of increasing the term of a contract; the actual term to be chosen depends on balancing these costs and benefits. A major advantage of longer-term contracts is that longer terms allow efficient investment in relationship-specific capital. Thus, one important point is that the greater the level of specific investment needed in a series of transactions, the greater the benefits of long-term contracts. Costs of making contracts longer term include the costs of anticipating what might occur in the future, deciding how to handle each of these contingencies, and drafting an enforceable contract to cover the eventualities. These costs would increase with uncertainty in the industry. Thus, in a stable industry with substantial specific investing, long-term contracts should be used. As these features change, shorter contracts become more desirable.

Even if contracts were complete and enforceable, it is better to avoid courts and litigation if possible. Litigation is time consuming and expensive. Outcomes are uncertain. In general, the most one can expect from successful litigation over a contract is a payment of damages, rather than *specific performance*. That is, in general, the courts will not order a party to perform on a contract as written, and even if they do, it may take a long time before litigation is over and performance can be ordered.* (Specific performance will often be ordered in contracts for the sale of a specific, named asset, such as a building at a certain location.) For

---

*Obviously, the issue is more complex, and this is a point which should be decided by an attorney.

business purposes, performance might be worth more than damages. In any event, litigation is to be avoided where possible.

This should not be taken to imply that firms should do business without a contract. Even though contracts are imperfect, they do have many useful functions. One of these is, of course, the threat of litigation for damages to prevent breach. This is particularly important because such a threat will generally serve to limit damages. Even if someone would not litigate for a breach which cost $1,000, he would for $10,000, so that threat of litigation serves as an incentive to limit harm caused by breach. Moreover, contracts are the only enforcement mechanisms that are always available. The other methods which we discuss below are often preferable when available, but each of them has limitations. However, it is useful to use other mechanisms other than contract wherever possible.

AN EASY CASE: MOBILE-SPECIFIC CAPITAL

Problems of potential opportunism occur only if there is a specific asset and internal production is impractical. A paradigm case would be a firm which needs a specially machined part but which is itself not in the metal-working business. The part is made by a machine shop which also makes many other parts for other customers (or else it would pay to buy the entire machine shop). If the part itself requires a special input—say, specialized tooling—and if this special input is portable, then the customer firm can simply own the die and contract with the machine shop to produce the required part using the buyer's die. Holdup problems are thus eliminated because if the machine shop should attempt to raise prices, the customer can immediately remove his die and contract with another machine shop for production. Thus, in the case of specialized assets which are physically mobile, ownership by the customer is feasible and can serve to eliminate the problems under discussion. This process can be observed in various industries.

Of course, there are costs to this arrangement as well. For example, the machine shop in this case may not have adequate incentives to maintain the die in good condition. The firm owning the die may have to assign an employee to work in the machine shop and supervise the maintenance of the die. This is an easy case. When the conditions specified are met, then firms can use this mechanism. However, it lacks generality. There will be many opportunities for holdup which lack the feature required for this mechanism to operate.

SELF-ENFORCING AGREEMENTS

In some cases, it is possible for firms to implicitly enter into a *self-enforcing agreement*. This is an agreement, for example, to buy a product, which has no third-party enforcement (such as the courts) associated with it. Since there is no external enforcement, the agreements are implicit; they are not in general written down. Each party abides by the agreement only so long as it pays to do so. The agreement is self-enforcing in that it will maintain itself with no need for outside interference. Because such agreements are self-maintaining and require little or no monitoring and enforcement, firms should try wherever possible to structure transactions as being self-enforcing.

A paradigm case would be an agreement for one firm to purchase some product from another. Firm S sells a product bought by Firm B. The product is specialized. Initially, both firms must make some investment in production. Firm B must spend resources in telling Firm S what it wants, and Firm S must set up an assembly line to produce the product. Because of these investments, B can buy the product more cheaply from S than from any competing seller, and S can get more from B than from any competing buyer.

B pays for the product upon delivery. If quality is unsatisfactory, B's only recourse is to cease transacting with S. S must spend substantial resources in producing and guaranteeing quality, perhaps by using expensive ingredients, or perhaps by spending large amounts on quality control. The price B pays is based on the value to B of high-quality goods. S can therefore make large profits in one production period by degrading quality and thus reducing costs and still collecting from B. However, after this one-shot profit, B will no longer buy from S and, because B is paying more than competing buyers (because of the investments undertaken by S) S will lose something on each lost future sale.

Therefore, in each production period S has two options. He may make a high-quality product and continue the relationship, thus gaining the future profits associated with this business. He can also behave opportunistically, degrade the product, and make a one-shot profit. However, this will result in losing the future profits from continuing the relationship. B wants to structure the transaction so that S will continue to participate.

The price chosen will be such that the expected future profits to S from continuing the transaction will be greater than the one-shot profits from cheating. This depends on the actual prices and also on the expected future life of the agreement absent cheating. A general proposition is that there must be some quasirents associated with the transaction in order to provide incentives for repeated and continuing transactions. These can arise because of relationship-specific investments of various sorts. That is, the selling firm may undertake some investment which will become worthless if the sequence of transactions ceases. This investment will generate a stream of payments, a quasirent, which will serve to guarantee the transaction. The goal is to make the short-run gains from cheating as low as possible and the long-run gains from continuing the relationship as large as possible. Throughout the book, we will see several applications of this general principle. There are certain additional principles of such agreements which can help guide managers in structuring such transactions.

First, consider the last period of the transaction. If S knows that there will be no more transactions after October 1991, what incentive does S have? Clearly, in October 1991, S will deliver low-quality merchandise since there is no future business to lose and there are profits to gain from opportunistic behavior in this period. But B knows that S will provide low quality in the last period, so B will not buy from S in October 1991. But S knows that B will not buy in October, so S treats September as the last period and will then deliver low-quality product in September. B will know this and will not buy anything in September. We can extend the same logic, month by month, back to the present. The process will *unravel*. This unravelling is a well-known phenomenon, associated with what is called a *last-period problem*. If there is a last period known to both parties, then no self-enforcing agreement of the sort described here will be feasible.

What is the solution? Clearly, the only viable solution for a self-enforcing agreement is to have no fixed termination date. When the arrangement is being established, under no circumstances should B tell S when the agreement will end. Moreover, if B should learn at some point that it will stop buying at a known date in the future, B should not communicate this date to S in advance either. If the nature of the transaction is such that a known ending date can be predicted by both parties, then this transaction is not a candidate for being operated as a self-enforcing agreement. B will need to rely either on an explicit contract, on internal production, or on other mechanisms discussed elsewhere. While all sequences of transactions will end at some point, the longer a sequence is expected to be, the more of a candidate it is for being treated as a self-enforcing agreement.

There are some other guidelines for such agreements. It might appear to B that a good past record on the part of S should be used to generate goodwill and excuse an occasional slip. However, this is not the case. B's only strategy is to immediately terminate the relationship if S ever supplies sufficiently low quality. If B does not do this, then S will be able to opportunistically exploit B by periodically offering low quality. B cannot let himself be open to such exploitation, and therefore cannot forgive any lapses. In the context of a self-enforcing agreement, "What have you done for me lately" is the watchword. This does not mean that any small error on the part of S will lead to cancellation, but it does mean that any large enough deviation should end the arrangement. (If S errs for reasons beyond his control, he can compensate B for the costs of the error and maintain the arrangement.)

Parties to a self-enforcing agreement will only enter such an agreement if they expect it to continue. It does not pay to begin such an arrangement with expectations of breach. Therefore, the agreement will end only if external conditions change, so such agreements are more profitable in industries or circumstances where there is relatively little uncertainty. As conditions are more uncertain, self-enforcing agreements are less likely.

Though there are limits to self-enforcing agreements, it is important to note that most business is done through such agreements. Most dealing between suppliers and their customers is on a relatively informal basis, and the major sanction for opportunism is simply the loss in future business. (As we shall see, this is also the basis of most dealing between retail establishments and consumers.) Self-enforcing agreements are common in transactions where neither party has invested (much) in relationship-specific capital. Thus, although the emphasis in this book is on cases where such agreements do not work, these are a minority of real world transactions—ones in which parties have invested in relationship-specific capital, while a minority of transactions, are generally the key transactions in the structure of a business.

"HOSTAGES"

One method of assuring performance is to offer a *"hostage"*—a valuable asset which will be forfeit if a contract or agreement is not honored. If the hostage is chosen correctly, then it is possible to obtain efficient contractual performance. Either party may be in a position to behave opportunistically with respect to the other, so either party might find it desirable to offer a hostage or credible commitment. The performing party, for example, might not perform, or might provide lower quality than agreed on. The paying party might not pay. Thus, either party might want to bind himself to do what is promised.

The most important hostage for guaranteeing performance is a stream of quasirents associated with some fixed investment in a transaction. This stream of quasirents will be lost if the relationship between the two firms is broken, so it serves as a hostage. This sort of hostage appears in many types of transactions.

Another type of hostage is a cash bond. A performing party establishes a bond which is to be forfeit if he does not perform. A related alternative is a stated damage payment for delayed or inadequate performance. The problem with a cash bond, however, is that the paying party may be in a position to hinder the performing party in fulfilling the contract, and a bond may make such hindrance profitable. Consider, for example, a contract to construct a building by a certain date with a damage payment for each day the product is late. The paying party controls the land and also the acceptance of the building. If the damage payment is too large (i.e., larger than the actual cost to the buyer of delay), the buyer may have an incentive to allege nonperformance. ("The building is not suitable in its current state because the air conditioning is inadequate.") The buyer may also be in a position to induce breach. For example, the buyer may know some fact which will affect the ability of the seller to complete the job on time, but may not tell the seller. (For example, access to the land is limited to five days per week, so that overtime will not be an option to the builder.)

SOME ADDITIONAL MECHANISMS

Perhaps for this reason, courts will not always enforce contracts with specified damage payments. But whether or not the contracts will be enforceable, before he signs such a contract, a manager should be aware of the incentives created for the other party to induce or allege breach in order to receive the payment. However, there are several alternative mechanisms which can sometimes solve this problem.

Sunk Investments

An alternative to a direct money payment is an investment which is sunk (i.e., already made) but which will not accrue to the other party.

For example, consider some transaction where the seller must invest in a specific asset in order to produce the product wanted by the buyer. (Assume that the asset is not moveable, so that the alternative discussed above, buyer ownership of the asset, is not feasible.) The danger is that the buyer will not buy as much as promised, so that the seller's investment will return less than anticipated. The seller, fearing this, will be reluctant to undertake the investment. The buyer would like to commit himself to buy enough to induce the seller to undertake the investment.

One option is a contract, with all the weaknesses associated with contracts and with third-party enforcement. Another option is for the buyer to invest in expensive specific capital which is only valuable if the buyer fulfills his commitments. We may call this *nonsalvageable* capital. For example, the buyer might establish a store and invest in it, so that he can say to the seller, "Of course I will buy all that I have agreed to. I have 4,000 square feet of shelf space to fill which will be worthless if I behave opportunistically and buy less."

Since the space will be wasted if the buyer reneges, there is no incentive for the seller to induce breach, as there would be if the buyer had posted a bond. However, this solution is not cost-free either. It may be, for example, that market conditions change so radically that the product really becomes worthless. In this case, the buyer will lose his investment and, unlike a cash bond, no one will gain the equivalent value. This type of solution is most useful in industries with relatively little uncertainty. We will see in Chapter 9 that the creation of hostages of just this sort is common when firms want to convince consumers of the quality of their products.

Mandatory Licensing

An additional mechanism, related to a hostage, is to require a seller of specialized technological inputs to license the relevant technology to other producers. This is essentially a requirement that manufacturers release a hostage, the license. Buyers of computer chips sometimes impose this requirement. It is aimed at preventing a holdup problem. Once a manufacturer is committed to a particular chip, familiar problems of potential hold up come into being. The requirement of licensing is a way of protecting against opportunism. The U.S. Department of Defense, as a buyer of military equipment, sometimes requires second sourcing for similar reasons, and often requires the prime source to share technology with others.

Price Constraints

Another alternative to forestall attempts to holdup is to bind one-self in such a way that giving in to an attempted holdup would be too costly. A "most favored nation" pricing clause can sometimes achieve this goal. A buyer stipulates in his contract with each seller that if he (the buyer) should renegotiate and pay *any* seller a higher price, then *every* seller will receive that same higher price. Each seller then knows that it would be very expensive indeed for the buyer to give in to an attempt at holdup, and as a result sellers are much less likely to attempt to appropriate any quasirents. Such clauses are sometimes seen in con-tracts between canners and fishermen or growers of produce, between pipelines and natural gas producers, and between unions and firms hiring union labor (where the union constrains itself to match any wage cut for one firm to all other firms). If a firm buys the same product from several suppliers, then this mechanism might be useful.

Bilateral Exchange

A very common method of guaranteeing performance in situations where either party might behave opportunistically is reciprocal ex-change. Each party buys some specialized product, or product requir-ing a specialized input, from the other and sells a similar product to the other. The reciprocal nature of the transactions automatically provides both parties with hostages to guarantee the behavior of the other.

Whether this technique will work depends on the nature of the goods used by the two parties, and in many circumstances it will not be feasible. Nonetheless, when feasible it is a very useful and efficient technique. Therefore, if a manager of Firm B is in a position of buying some specialized input from Firm S and is afraid that S will behave opportunistically, he should look for something for B to sell to S which will make it possible for Firm B to also behave opportunistically. Con-versely, if he is selling to a firm which is afraid of being the victim of opportunism, then the solution might be to offer to buy from the other firm, thus improving the terms of the transaction.

For example, many firms produce linerboard and corrugating medium, the two components of corrugated cardboard boxes. Because firms may not produce both components in the proportions needed for producing cardboard, and because geographic distribution of produc-tion and consumption may differ, firms often need one product or the other from other firms. One way to obtain needed supplies would be through market transactions. However, this would put the firm buying the product at the mercy of the firm selling. As a result, the standard method of transacting in this market is direct exchange: Firm A will trade linerboard for medium from Firm B, or linerboard in Georgia for linerboard in Oregon. Since these exchanges are reciprocal, neither firm is in a position to hold up the other without putting itself in exactly the same position.

Joint Venture

One extreme form of bilateral exchange is the creation of a joint venture. This occurs when two enterprises create a third which is jointly owned by the first two. This is a powerful mechanism, but its application is limited. It is most feasible when the product of the exchanges between the two parties is itself a substantial product which has its own market and which has minimal interactions (in the form of economies of scale or economies of scope) with other products. The market must be sufficiently large to justify creation of a new firm. In this case, the jointly owned venture is itself a hostage for both parties. Any attempt by either party to exploit the venture will impose costs on both parties since both own the assets of the joint venture. Thus, this structure by its very nature reduces possibilities for opportunism.

Sometimes it is possible to build additional safeguards into the contract forming the joint venture. Assume that the venture is formed by S, the seller, and B, the buyer. The seller is worried that the buyer will buy from some third party, and thus make his investment worthless. If each party has 50 percent representation on the board of directors of the joint venture, then the seller can protect himself by requiring a supermajority for making a purchasing decision. If all purchasing decisions involving the product of S require a 60 percent vote of the board, there is no way in which S can be exploited by the venture. Such contractual mechanisms can strengthen the limits on opportunism associated with the creation of the joint venture, but of course the circumstances where this mechanism will be feasible are limited.

Reputation

In one sense, the most important guarantee available is the reputation of one's trading partner. A reputation for not behaving opportunistically is very valuable under certain circumstances, and a firm with such a reputation would have strong incentives not to cheat and lose this asset. As a manager, it may pay for you to invest substantial amounts in creating such a reputation. Chapter 8 deals directly with methods available to a firm for enhancing its reputation. However, note at this point that a reputation is valuable only if a firm can capitalize on it. This means that the firm must be able to make a profit on sales for a reputation to be valuable.

If you are buying some product, you may have two options. One is to buy from a relatively new and low-cost firm which lacks a reputation. The other may be to pay a premium for a product from an established firm with a good reputation. One strategy is to spread purchases, and buy relatively less critical goods from the new firm. This will result in cost savings and will generate information about the reputation of the new firm, which may be valuable later. It may also be that you have particular knowledge of a new supplier who has not yet developed a reputation. In this case, you can profit on your particular knowledge by buying from this new, unknown (to the market) supplier.

A firm which is owned by a single individual has a difficult problem. An individual has a finite life. As he becomes older, the value of his reputation becomes less because there is a shorter time period over which to earn returns on his reputation. (This is an example of the last-period problem, discussed above.) If the firm is the family business however, where children are involved, the life of the firm extends beyond the life of the founder. Another possibility is for the owner to sell the firm, so that the new buyer will have an incentive to preserve the reputation. A corporation has no determinate life span, so that this problem does not arise in this context.

MONITORING

In addition to attempting to structure the exchange so as to provide incentives for efficient behavior, it will generally be useful to monitor the behavior of the other party to try to reduce losses from any shirking which may occur. The theory developed here has several implications for such monitoring.

First, you should look for changes in the condition of your trading partner. At the time a contract is signed, it is in the interests of both parties to obey the terms of the contract. However, if conditions change, then incentives may change in predictable ways. For an important example, if a firm is experiencing financial difficulty, then it may pay for the firm to engage in additional opportunistic behavior. If, for an extreme case, the firm will go bankrupt unless it cheats, then the incentives for cheating become much more substantial because the reputation of the firm will become worthless anyway if it shuts down. Therefore, it may pay to monitor the financial health of any firms which have a critical relationship with your firm.

Second, there will sometimes be an option as to monitoring inputs or outputs of trading partners, where the output of your supplier is your input. Monitoring of inputs will occur if you observe, for example, the quality of raw materials which your supplier uses. Monitoring of outputs will occur if you simply observe the product you are receiving, which is the output of your trading partner. It will generally be cheaper and easier to monitor outputs since you must do some inspection of received goods as part of normal use. If transactions are frequent and relatively small, then monitoring of outputs will usually be adequate. However, if transactions are large and infrequent, then it may pay to monitor inputs since in this circumstance, by the time low quality is detected it may be too late to do anything about the opportunism. For example, if a crop is harvested once a year and is an input into your production process (you run a canning factory), then you may want to be sure that your suppliers are growing high-quality products because if you do not monitor, then by the time you find out that they are not, it will be too late.

Third, there may be advantages to dealing with a relatively small number of suppliers. One such advantage is reduced monitoring, particularly monitoring of the general reputation and financial health of the firm. A second advantage may come about because a supplier selling many materials to the same customer will have an incentive not to behave opportunistically since such behavior, if detected, will cause losses in many dimensions.

Fourth, you should realize that your supplier may have problems monitoring his own employees. To the extent possible, you should attempt to determine controls which your trading partner has imposed on his employees in those areas where employee opportunism can effect you. In some circumstances, for example, it may be better to deal with a local supplier rather with than a branch of a distant firm because monitoring of its employees by the supplier may be easier.

Finally, it will sometimes be possible to enlist a third party to assist in monitoring suppliers. One possibility is a trade association which provides incentives for or certifies honest behavior. Another possibility is obtaining a performance bond from an insurance company. This will protect you from failure by your partner. Such bonds can be used only in limited circumstances, as where the characteristics of the product are easily measurable. However, in the circumstances where they are feasible, they can be useful. Such bonds are particularly useful for new or untried firms. If you are dealing with such a firm, you might suggest obtaining such a bond. If you are a manager in such a firm, you might offer to obtain a bond.

INTRAFIRM TRANSACTIONS

So far, we have been dealing with transactions between firms. However, for firms with many divisions, there are often transfers of products between divisions. Such transfers may create agency problems of opportunism and shirking of the same sort we have discussed. Generally in such transfers there are three parties involved: the heads of the two divisions and the CEO of the company. Since division heads are rated, paid, and promoted on the basis of their performance, issues of the terms of transfers are significant. The essence of the agency problem is establishing terms of exchange and reward structures so that each division manager, in maximizing his own return, will also maximize profits for the firm. In such transactions, there are two important issues: the choice of a supplier (i.e., whether the buying division will buy from the selling division or from an outside supplier) and the transfer price. Several mechanisms are available for controlling agency problems in this context.

Simulating a Market

One option is a market-like contract. The two divisions (S, the selling division, and B, the buying division) will deal with each other in ways similar to independent firms. This will generally imply that each division has the option to buy or sell outside, in addition to dealing with the other division. This sort of contract is most common in highly diversified companies where there are few interrelationships between divisions. In such companies, it may actually be more difficult for divisions to deal with each other than would be the case for independent firms because there are conflicting incentives. Managers of both divisions may seek to be promoted, and promotion prospects may depend on the relative profitably of the divisions. Therefore, if B pays a higher price to S, this will not only make B worse off by reducing its profits, but may also make B worse off by making S relatively better off. (This issue is discussed below, in Chapter 3, dealing with "contests" as a method of determining promotions.)

Since simulation of a market cannot do better than actual use of a market, and may do worse because of internal conflicts, we may ask why this technique is used. However, this leads to a more fundamental question: If two divisions have no closer relationship than two independent firms and if there are costs but no benefits from coordinating their behavior through command rather than through market transactions, then why are they in the same firm? One possible answer is that these divisions have additional relationships with other divisions of the firm. However, another answer may be that there is no reason for the two divisions to be in the same firm. As seen below (Chapter 5), there are incentives for firms to expand in inefficient directions, and sometimes to become too large. If there are many divisions in a firm which deal with each other only through market-like transactions and which have no other complimentarities, this may be a sign that exactly this sort of overexpansion has occurred.

(In the appendix to this chapter, two schemes are proposed for devising transfer prices and policies between divisions which have desirable theoretical properties, but which have not been tested in practice.)

Hierarchial Structure

In a hierarchial structure of internal exchange, the selling division will essentially be subordinate to the buying division. The buying division will function as a profit center (evaluated by its contribution to profits for the enterprise), while the selling division will function as a cost center (evaluated by its ability to meet its goals without exceeding its budget). Cost centers are likely to be divisions whose output is difficult to measure quantitatively. Evaluation of the performance of the selling division will then be in terms of its efficiency in reducing costs of production and in supplying the amount and quality of input needed by the buying division. Since the buying and selling divisions will together function as a team, as discussed in Chapter 3, there is no direct measure of the marginal product or performance of the selling division.

For this structure, rewards depend on direct monitoring of the efficiency and performance of each party. This requires knowledge by top management of the functions and constraints facing each party to the transaction. This is apparently a more difficult requirement than monitoring based on market simulation, discussed above. Nonetheless, it may be more efficient only because in those situations where perfect market-like monitoring is feasible, the divisions should probably be separate anyway. If there are no gains to internal coordination, then managers should use the most powerful techniques for cost control, and direct use of the market is the most powerful incentive.

SUMMARY

Vertical integration, as discussed in the last chapter, is one solution to potential opportunism. However, there will be circumstances under which this will not be feasible and firms will transact with each other even though there are possibilities for opportunism. In this chapter, several possible mechanisms for reducing or solving this problem were discussed. In all cases, it is important to remember that both parties have an incentive to make the transaction as efficient as possible since this will increase the amount to be divided between the parties.

We have identified several methods of reducing opportunism. One is the use of contracts and court enforcement, which is often useful and necessary, but should nonetheless be viewed as a last resort. A second method is for the buying firm to own the specialized capital used by the selling firm. This is a good solution where it is feasible, but the requirements—that the capital be easily moved—are restrictive, and the application is limited. A third possibility is to attempt to structure the contract as being self-enforcing. Again, where feasible, this is a desirable mechanism. It requires, among other conditions, that there be no fixed ending date for the transaction. Most real world business dealings are of this sort. Another possibility is the use of a "hostage," which a firm can offer or demand. This can be in the form of money payments, although these create problems since they may give the other party an incentive to allege or induce breach. The firm may also invest in some nonsalvageable capital which gives it an incentive to fulfill its agreement. Where feasible, firms may engage in reciprocal exchanges so that each has an automatic performance bond with respect to the other. One example of such reciprocal exchange is the creation of a joint venture involving the two firms. Returns on investments in transaction-specific capital generate a stream of quasirents, and the potential loss of these quasirents serves to guarantee performance. Another important guarantor of performance is a valuable reputation, and firms should sometimes invest in acquiring such a reputation.

As should be clear, the only technique always available is the explicit written contract with reliance on the courts for enforcement. This method of enforcement has disadvantages, and when all other techniques fail the firm should consider or reconsider the possibility of vertical integration. Nonetheless, of course, contracts will still be used in numerous situations.

Two techniques for controlling transactions between divisions within the firm are market techniques and direct hierarchial control. At first, it may appear that use of market-like techniques is most efficient since markets have many desirable properties. However, if such techniques are easy to use between two divisions, then this is an indication that the firm is probably overinclusive. If two divisions can interact efficiently only through market-like mechanisms, then they should probably be independent and actually use the market. This means that for those interactions which should actually take place within a firm, hierarchial controls and direct monitoring are the correct (although difficult) control techniques.

REFERENCES

Clarkson, Kenneth W., Miller, Roger L., and Muris, Timothy J. "Liquidated Damages v. Penalties: Sense or Nonsense." *Wisconsin Law Review* (1987) 351.

Eccles, Robert G. "Transfer Pricing as a Problem of Agency." In *Principles and Agents: The Structure of Business,* edited by John W. Pratt and Richard J. Zeckhauser. Boston: Harvard Business School Press, 1985.

Hart, Oliver. "Incomplete Contracts." In *Allocation, Information, and Markets,* (from *The New Palgrave*), edited by John Eatwell, Murray Milgate, and Peter Newman. Norton, 1987, 1989.

Heimer, Carol A. *Reactive Risk and Rational Action: Managing Moral Hazard in Insurance Contracts.* Berkeley: University of California Press, 1985.

Knoeber, Charles R. "An Alternative Mechanism to Assure Contractual Reliability." *Journal of Legal Studies* 12 (1983): 333.

Macaulay, Stewart. "Non-Contractual Relations in Business." *American Sociological Review* 28 (1963): 55.

Monteverde, Kirk, and Teece, David J. "Appropriable Rents and Quasi-Vertical Integration." *Journal of Law and Economics* 25 (1982):321.

Rubin, Paul H. "Unenforceable Contracts: Penalty Clauses and Specific Performance." *Journal of Legal Studies* 10 (1981):69. Reprinted in *Business Firms and the Common Law,* edited by Paul Rubin. New York: Praeger, 1983.

Shavell, Steven. "The Design of Contracts and Remedies for Breach." *Quarterly Journal of Economics* 99 (1984): 121.

Telser, Lester G. "A Theory of Self-Enforcing Agreements." *The Journal of Business* 53 (Jan. 1980): 27.

Williamson, Oliver,. *The Economic Institutions of Capitalism,* chapters 7–8. New York: Free Press, 1985.

Williamson, Oliver. "Transaction Cost Economics." In *Handbook of Industrial Organization,* edited by Richard Schmalensee and Robert Willig. New York: North Holland, 1989.

APPENDIX
Transfer Price Schemes

In this appendix, I suggest a scheme for governing transactions involving divisions which are themselves profit centers, and a scheme for allocating a joint venture between the venturers. However, before setting out the schemes, the reader should note one important caveat. In most of the rest of this book, proposals for managerial policies are based on ideas or schemes which have actually been observed in real situations, or on straightforward modifications of such schemes. The proposals in this appendix are for schemes which have been devised by theorists. So far as I am aware, they have not been used in real firms. Therefore, before adopting either of these proposals, you should consider carefully all of the implications. Nonetheless, the schemes have such desirable properties that they are worth discussing. The first proposal is for a mechanism determining if transactions between divisions are worthwhile. The second is for allocating a joint venture after it will no longer be joint.

INTERDIVISIONAL TRANSFERS

There are two divisions, a buying division and a selling division. The buying division must place a valuation on the product; the selling division must place a cost. The mechanism is as follows:

1. The buying division reports its value of the good, B.

2. The selling division reports its cost of the good, C.

3. If $B > C$ (i.e., if the value the buying division places on the good is greater than the cost the selling division reports) then headquarters charges C to the buying division, credits the selling division with B, and transfers one unit of the good from the seller to the buyer. (Note that the payment to each party depends on the valuation of the other party.)

4. If $B < C$ (i.e., if the value the buying division places on the good is less than the cost the selling division reports) then there is no transfer.

This mechanism has the following properties: First, both divisions will report true prices because it is in their interest to do so. This is because for each division the price it pays is determined by the valuation of the other division. If the buying division reported a value less than the true value of the good, then sometimes there would be no transaction even if it were in the interests of the buying division. Since the value reported by the buying division does not affect the price received by that division (and vice versa for the selling division), but only whether or not there is a transaction, there is no gain to the buying division from misreporting. If it reports a price below its true valuation, then there may not be a transaction, but if there is, the actual price it pays is not affected. The reciprocal analysis applies to the selling division. Both parties have an incentive to report truthfully.

Second, transactions should occur only if $B > C$, and this mechanism does guarantee this. If $B < C$, this means that the value to the buying division is less than the cost to the selling division of making the product (or less than the opportunity cost of selling it elsewhere) and, therefore, there should be no transaction. If $B > C$, then there should be a transaction because the value to the buying division is greater than the cost to the selling division. Thus, this mechanism does have certain desirable properties. It leads to transactions occurring when it is in the interest of the firm, and to no transactions when it is not.

There are, however, some disadvantages. For one thing, note that the profits credited to the two divisions are greater than the total firm profit (except in the special case where $B = C$), since headquarters makes up the difference. Thus, profits of the divisions cannot be used to measure total firm profits, nor can the managers of these divisions be compared with managers of other divisions whose internal accounting profits are based on other mechanisms.

Second, there are possibilities of the two divisions colluding against headquarters. If the buying division reports a much greater valuation than its true value, then the selling division will receive a larger payment. (Similarly, the same occurs for the buying division if the selling division understates costs.) Since these are only internal accounting transactions, there is no way the selling division can repay the buying division in money for the overvaluation, so the gains from collusion are limited. However, if there are additional transactions between the divisions, there may be possibilities for gains. For example, the selling division could "loan" the buying division some personnel which were charged to the selling division as a repayment for the buying division's overstating its valuation. Thus, this scheme is most feasible where there are minimal additional transactions between the divisions, and perhaps where there is actual geographic separation between them.

ALLOCATING A JOINT VENTURE

Assume that two firms are contemplating a joint venture which entails some investment in fixed capital and which will be approximately equally owned by the two firms. (This mechanism will also work for dissolving a partnership.) At some point the venture will be dissolved and it will then be necessary to allocate the asset to one of the two firms. It is contemplated that the asset will be worth more to one of these two firms than to any outside bidder (or else it could be sold and the proceeds split), but it is not now known which will value it most. In order to provide proper incentives for the investment, firms must anticipate that they will receive something for the asset when it is sold. It is also in the interests of both that the asset ultimately be allocated to the firm which will place the highest value on it since this will create the largest surplus to be split.

There is a mechanism which will accomplish this set of goals. At the time of dissolution, each firm indicates some value of the asset to itself. Let H be the value which the firm placing a higher value on the asset will announce, and L be the value of the firm with the lower value. Then H will receive the asset. Firm L will be paid compensation of one-third H by the winning firm.

In this scheme, each party will have an incentive to state his exact value of the item. If a party understates his true valuation, he may lose the good and the expected loss is greater than the expected saving from understatement. If a party overstates his valuation and gets the good, then he gains less than his gain from receiving one-third of the other party's valuation (and saving one-third of his own valuation). Both parties have incentives to tell the truth, and the good will go to the party with the highest valuation. If the parties can agree on this method of allocating the good before the venture is begun, then there will be an efficient investment in the venture.

These schemes have not been tried. Overall, however, the mechanisms are promising. One strategy is to use a mechanism experimentally for a period and observe the results. The theoretical basis is strong enough so that it may be worth an attempt at use.

REFERENCES

Radner, Roy. "The Internal Economy of Large Firms." *Economic Journal* 96 (Supplement, 1986):1.

Myerson, Roger B. "Mechanism Design." In *Allocation, Information, and Markets* (from *The New Palgrave*), edited by John Eatwell, Murray Milgate, and Peter Newman. New York: Norton, 1987, 1989.

– 3 –

Structuring Employment Agreements

Workers are an input into the production process. Therefore, the general principles involved in devising efficient devices for labor arrangements are similar to those raised in the last two chapters with respect to inputs in general. In devising contracts or arrangements for paying and motivating workers, the goals are to make arrangements which maximize the output of the worker net of costs. By creating the largest total net output, the firm creates the largest amount to be split between the employer and the employee.

This desire for efficiency in the wage contract should be particularly obvious to a manager, for the manager is both an employer of workers (in his role as a supervisor) and an employee. In reading this chapter, therefore, the manager should look for two things: (1) devices which will enable him to better manage those workers under his supervision because this will increase his productivity as a manager; and (2) devices or mechanisms which he can propose to his supervisor to increase his own productivity because this will increase his value as a worker and therefore his wage.

THEORY OF AGENCY

The general issue to be considered in devising labor contracts (whether explicit or implicit) is that the goals of workers and employers will not be congruent. To a greater or lesser extent, workers will pursue their own goals rather than the goals of the firm. Workers can do this because information is not perfect. If a manager observes a bad outcome (say, low sales from some salesman), the manager cannot always tell if the unfavorable outcome is due to worker shirking or to unfortunate conditions in the market, such as a reduction in demand for the product.

This lack of congruence will have costs, called *agency costs.* These costs are of three types. First are the costs associated with the reduction in output caused by the divergence. Second, employers will spend resources trying to reduce the amount of divergence, although in general it will not pay to reduce it to zero even if this is technologically possible. Third, the workers themselves will spend resources to reduce this divergence between their goals and the firm's goals, for if a worker can convince his employer that he is a "better" worker, his pay will increase.

The worker analog to opportunism is *shirking,* which is the cause of agency costs between employees and employers. Shirking can take many forms, from mild laziness to outright theft. A worker may simply not work as hard as he should; he may work hard on tasks which are in his, but not his employer's, interest; he may misuse the employer's resources, as by making personal long-distance phone calls; he may accept bribes from, for example, suppliers; or he may engage in actual theft.

One example of shirking is the acceptance of bribes from vendors by purchasing agents. A purchasing agent accepting such bribes would choose goods and services for the firm based on his own benefits, rather than on costs and benefits to the firm. This is the essence of shirking.

A timely example is conflict arising from "frequent-flyer" programs offered by airlines. Here an employee (the traveller) has substantial control over his own travel schedule and often can choose the carrier. Frequent-flyer plans benefit travellers who fly on certain airlines and, sometimes, who stay in certain hotel chains or rent cars from particular auto rental agencies. In all cases, the bonus is a transfer in kind, commonly in additional travel. An alternative would be a direct cash transfer. However, a cash transfer would probably be claimed by the company, which, after all, is paying for the travel. Airlines actually make it difficult for employers to determine the amount of mileage that an employee has accumulated.

There are inefficiencies (agency costs) associated with frequent-flyer programs. Some travellers may take extra, unneeded, trips at the employer's expense. Even for trips which are needed, travellers may schedule flights based on their frequent-flyer program, rather than cost or work-associated convenience. Airlines have created an agency problem between workers and firms in their creation of frequent-flyer programs.

In the short run, workers benefit from these programs. However, the long-term effect is likely to be reduction in income for those employees who travel substantial amounts. Employees will accept this implicit pay reduction because they will benefit from the free trips. However, "income in kind" (free travel) is always worth less than income in money. Money could be used to buy either travel or other goods and services, so the employee can be no better off receiving travel (neglecting tax considerations) and may be worse off. Overall, the programs will reduce the real incomes of those workers who travel extensively.

Nonetheless, it may not pay for firms to spend the resources needed to effectively monitor employee behavior. Some firms are doing so, but these are large firms requiring substantial amounts of travel. One alternative is to make all employees belong to all frequent-flyer plans, so that the distortion caused by the plans will be reduced, although since payoffs grow faster than miles travelled, this will not eliminate the inefficiency.

Another form of shirking is spending time and effort on what has been called "influence activities." These are attempts by workers to influence superiors to give them better jobs, working conditions, or other benefits. Such activities are inefficient from the perspective of the firm because time spent on influence is not spent on work and, thus, is unproductive. However, it is possible to design a firm to minimize this inefficiency. In particular, it may be useful to have many decisions made through rules rather than managerial discretion. This will be especially true of decisions where there is little effect on the firm but much effect on worker satisfaction. For example, rules which allocate office space based solely on seniority can be efficient because they reduce incentives for using influence to obtain a better office.

Employers will spend resources policing shirking, but in general they will not reduce the level to zero since this is not worthwhile. Any attempt to do this would be more costly than any potential gains, so we may say that there is an optimal amount of shirking. Employers may reduce shirking by various forms of direct monitoring, including outside monitoring such as the use of auditors.

An important element in reducing shirking is the structure of the contract (actual or implicit) between workers and firms. The general principle is that contracts should be written to make the goals of workers as close as possible to the goals of firms. Payments to workers should be related as closely as feasible to those aspects of worker behavior which benefit the employer.

An extreme method of eliminating shirking is simply to use the outside labor market to perform each task. Just as the open market is the major force providing cost discipline for suppliers, so it is the major force reducing incentives for shirking by workers. If a firm can specify a job exactly and easily determine whether it is done correctly or not, then the firm need not hire the worker as an employee to perform the job. Rather, the job can be put out for bid and the lowest cost bidder hired for the job. For example, in most large cities law firms and others commonly communicate by messengers. In general, these messengers are not employees of the law firms. Rather, the service is hired out. We may call such hiring out "contract labor" hired on a "piece-rate" basis. Competition among those providing messenger services keeps costs as low as possible for this service. Policing is done by the bidding process in the market, and the hiring firm need not spend any of its own resources on monitoring or policing.

Hiring of contract labor on a piece-rate basis is one extreme method of reducing shirking. Next is hiring of workers as employees paid on a strict productivity basis, as in a piecework contract. Under such a contract, workers would know that any shirking would reduce their output and thus their earnings, and therefore they would bear a large fraction of the cost. (The messengers discussed above work for messenger firms. They are not self-employed, but are paid on a strict piecework basis, so their earnings are closely related to their productivity.) In this circumstance, there would be relatively little shirking. There would still be some shirking since the worker does not get the full value of the product, but there would be less than with alternative schemes. Moreover, monitoring is relatively straightforward, since it consists mainly of counting output. As we will see, for many labor tasks, direct monitoring of output is not feasible, so that other contracts must be devised.

If it is easy to observe shirking, then a payment based simply on hours worked will be efficient. In an assembly line, a worker must produce as many units as go by his station, so an hourly wage is an efficient payment method in this context. In general, one determinant of the form of the contract will be the relative ease of monitoring inputs and outputs.

WHY NOT PAY ENTIRELY ON PRODUCTIVITY?

Most labor contracts do not take these extreme forms. Rather, most employees are paid a salary which is somewhat related to output and performance, but not nearly so closely as the above discussion would indicate. Any payment schedule which weakens the link between productivity and pay creates agency and shirking costs. Therefore, there must be some benefit associated with such contracts. Before we can discuss principles of optimal contract design, we must determine what these benefits are. There are several sorts.

Risk Aversion

One disadvantage of strict piecework contracts is that such contracts place large risks on workers. This is particularly true where the outcome of some effort depends in part on random factors not subject to control by the worker and not measurable by the employer. For example, sales of some product may depend on general economic conditions, or on conditions in the salesman's region, or on fashion, or on other factors not under the salesman's control. Therefore, a payment contract based solely on output would impose risks on the employee. Most employees are *risk averse,* meaning that they must be compensated to bear risk.

Consider the following problem: Employers are willing to pay up to 10 percent of sales to salesmen. Salesmen are risk averse, and willing to give up as much as $2,000 in expected earnings in order to avoid risk. Employers, because they are dealing with many salesmen, are risk neutral with respect to each. Assume initially that there are two contracts, a risk-free contract and a risky (from the perspective of the employee) contract. The risky contract creates additional incentives to avoid shirking, but requires a larger expected payment because of the employee's risk aversion.

For the risky contract, assume that a salesman is on 10 percent commission and might sell either $150,000 or $250,000, with equal probabilities, depending on economic conditions in his territory, if there is no shirking. There is then a 50 percent chance of earning $15,000 and a 50 percent chance of earning $25,000, so that the expected earnings are $20,000. With no shirking, the outcome depends on factors totally out of the control of the worker. Moreover, the employer cannot tell whether low sales are due to bad conditions or to shirking. The meaning of risk aversion is that most people would be willing to accept a lower, guaranteed payment rather than this riskier "lottery" of $15,000 or $25,000, even though the lottery has a higher expected value. We have assumed that an employee in this situation would be willing to give up $2,000 to avoid risk, so that the employee would be indifferent between $18,000 with certainty and the risky contract with an expected value of $20,000. If the employer wants the employee to bear the risk, he must pay the employee for doing this. In this example, the $2,000 is a risk premium which the worker demands for accepting the risk. This payment reduces the employer's returns. However, the employer might prefer the risky but more expensive contract if it provides better motivation for the worker.

If the employer could determine whether conditions were good or bad, he could pay the worker accordingly, without using the risky contract. That is, he could pay the worker $18,500 if either the worker sold $150,000 in a bad year or if the worker sold $250,000 in a good year. This would be preferred over the risky contract by the worker, who would have no risk, and by the employer, who would save $1,500. However, there are many real situations in which the employer cannot determine the true state of affairs. This example itself is obviously simplified because of the assumption of only two outcomes. In reality, of course, there would be a continuum of outcomes depending on economic conditions and worker effort, and neither would be observable by the employer.

Since employers hire many workers, employers are more likely to behave as if they are risk neutral with respect to any one employee, because they diversify risk over many employees. In any given year, half of the employees may sell $150,000 and half $250,000, so the contract which is risky to the employee will be less risky to the employer. As a result, all else equal, the employer would prefer to assume the risk himself and reduce the amount which he must pay the workers.

This does not mean that contracts imposing risk on workers could never be used. All else is not necessarily equal. In particular, it may be that for some jobs, the costs of shirking more than outweigh the risk premium. For example, in the above case, assume that if a worker were paid a salary he would shirk and sell $140,000 if times are bad and $200,000 in a good year (instead of the $150,000 and $250,000 if there is no shirking). If he were paid on the same percentage basis, then his income would be only $17,000. In this case, the risky contract would be preferred since the cost of shirking, $3,000, is greater than the risk premium, $2,000. That is, the worker would prefer $18,000 to the risky contract. However, if he does not accept the risky contract he can be paid only $17,000, because without the risky contract there is no way to provide incentives against shirking. As a result, the worker would end up choosing the risky contract.

Such risky contracts are common in situations where policing of behavior by the firm is very expensive or difficult. For example, many outside salesmen are paid entirely through commissions. Many such salesmen are technically not even employees of the firm but rather are "manufacturers' representatives," and technically self-employed. Monitoring of employees who are on the road is difficult and shirking would be a severe problem, so for these employees the risk premium is less than the shirking premium and a pure incentive contract is most efficient.

Even in this case, however, it may be possible to devise a better (although more complicated) contract. For example, consider the following contract: The employee is paid $15,900 plus 16 percent of any sales over $200,000. In any year in which he sells less than $150,000, he makes nothing, since it is known that sales less than this are solely due to shirking. There will never be sales of less than $150,000 under the assumptions given.

With this contract, in a bad year the employee makes $15,900, which is better for the employee than the $15,000 under a pure incentive contract. In a good year, he sells $250,000 and makes $23,900 ($15,900 plus 16 percent of $50,000), which is worse than the $25,000 under the pure incentive contract. His expected earnings are $19,900, so that the employer has saved $100 ($20,000 minus $19,900). But the employee may be happier as well because his worst case is now $15,900, rather than $15,000 and the employee may be willing to give up $100 in expected income for a guarantee of an extra $900 in a bad year. (See Table 1.)

The details of the example depend on the particular assumptions made, and are not important. In real world problems, the exact magnitudes will depend on the level of risk aversion of the employee and other details. What is interesting is that, in many situations, complicated payment schedules may both motivate employees and reduce risk below what it otherwise would be. These complicated schedules will often be two-part schedules, with a fixed payment and a charge based on output. In this example, the employee earns $16,000 for sales up to $200,000, and then his earnings increase as a percentage of sales. Another feature is that payment for the marginal contribution is higher than with other, more routine payment schedules. Here, for example, compensation on sales over $200,000 is 15 percent, rather than the 10 percent discussed earlier.

Notice that these compensation plans based on incentives are similar to common schemes for reducing costs of insurance, such as medical insurance. Commonly these plans have a coinsurance portion. That is, those covered by such plans pay a certain percentage of all

TABLE 1: Compensation Plans

Assumptions:

Probability of a good year = probability of a bad year = 50%
Sales in a "good" year with no shirking: $250,000
Sales in a "bad" year with no shirking: $150,000
Sales in a good year with shirking: $200,000
Sales in a bad year with shirking: $140,000

Initial Plan, Worker Bears Risk:

Commission rate: 10%
Income in a good year, no shirking: $25,000
Income in a bad year, no shirking, $15,000
Expected income under risky compensation, no shirking:
    .5($25,000) + .5($15,000) = $20,000
Income in a good year, shirking: $20,000
Income in a bad year, shirking: $14,000
Expected earnings under risky compensation, shirking:
    .5($20,000) + .5($14,000) = $17,000
By assumption, the risk premium demanded for accepting the risky package is
    $2,000. The cost of the nonrisky package is $3,000 because of shirking, so the
    risky package will be chosen.

Alternative Plan:

Payment equals $15,900 plus 16% of all sales over $200,000 (No income if sales
    are less than $150,000, implying shirking)
    Income in a good year: $15,900 + .16($50,000) = $23,900
    Income in a bad year: $15,900
Expected earnings under alternative compensation:
    .5($23,900) + .5(15,900) = $19,900
Employer has saved $100. Employee has lost expected income of $100, but has
    reduced risk. His lowest income is now $15,900, which is $900 more than un-
    der the pure risk compensation scheme.

medical costs. Such coinsurance increases the risk borne by the insured (and so acts like a commission rate) but also reduces the total cost of insurance by providing incentives for efficient use.

The tradeoff between risk and incentives is a general business phenomenon and managers should be aware of it and its possible ramifications. The type of contract discussed here is called a *two-part tariff*, which is a payment schedule with a fixed payment and a variable payment. The fixed payment is approximately equal to the expected value of the transaction, and the variable payment is used to provide incentives. Some examples of payment schedules following this scheme are: deductibles and coinsurance in automobile, casualty, and health insurance plans; franchise fees and additional payments based on sales (discussed in Chapter 7); and certain classes of agency contracts for sale of assets, discussed below. It is also possible to couple this type of contract with a penalty, such as the termination of the relationship if sales become sufficiently low as to provide convincing evidence of shirking. In general, there are many possibilities for use of such contracts, and some evidence that business does not use these contracts in all possible cases, and so misses some profitable opportunities. As a manager, you should be aware of the possibilities associated with this type of contract.

There is sometimes an additional benefit to a risky contract, or any contract which makes pay a function of output. A worker who plans to shirk or who knows that he will not be good at a job will be less likely to accept a job with such a contract. Therefore, by offering a contract with a significant penalty for low performance, an employer can get workers to self-select for a willingness to work hard, an example of a principle introduced in the last chapter.

Specialized Skills and Training

One explanation for labor contracts which reduce incentives inefficiently is risk aversion, discussed above. A second explanation is that workers sometimes have specialized training, more valuable in one firm than in any other. Such training is incompatible with piecework contracts and complete market incentives. Just as physical assets may be specialized for use in a particular firm, so may labor be specialized. The specialization of labor occurs through training, or acquisition of what is called "human capital." It is important to understand various types of human capital.

A useful distinction exists between *specific* and *general* human capital. General human capital is training and education which is useful in many firms. Specific human capital, which will generate specialized resources, is useful in only one firm. An example of general human capital is literacy; an example of specific human capital is knowledge of an idiosyncratic computer system, used in one particular firm.

Because general training is valuable in more than one firm, firms will not pay for acquiring it. Rather, workers themselves finance the acquisition of general training, most of which is acquired in schools. When firms provide general training, it is commonly paid for by workers themselves. This payment usually consists of accepting reduced wages during the period of training. Formal or informal apprenticeship programs provide a good example. (Some firms do pay tuition for, e.g., M.B.A. night programs. This is more properly viewed as a fringe benefit than as an investment in human capital for the firm's benefit, although the firm will benefit somewhat since some workers will remain with the firm.)

Specific capital raises different issues. Once a worker has acquired this capital, it is a specialized resource, valuable only in one firm. As such, it raises all the problems associated with any specialized asset. In particular, there is an associated quasirent, which may be appropriated. Relatively permanent labor contracts rather than pure-market contracting are used to avoid this appropriation.

A worker with some specific and some general human capital is worth no more in the market than the same worker with only the general human capital, so the firm need not pay any wage premium for the specific human capital. The result is that normally the firm will pay for acquisition of specific human capital. That is, the firm will pay the actual costs of providing whatever training (either explicit or on the job) is associated with the specific capital. Moreover, during the period when the worker is acquiring this capital, his market wage (from another firm) may be higher than his actual value to the firm, but the firm will pay this market wage. This overpayment is also part of the financing of the acquisition of human capital. Because this capital is paid for by the firm but embodied in and controlled by the worker, it produces quasirents which are subject to appropriation. (The section on bonding discusses some mechanisms available to limit this appropriation and other types of shirking.)

In most cases workers will pay for general human capital. However, there are some types of such capital for which workers cannot pay. This is "proprietary" information of various sorts. For example, it may take one hour to instruct an employee in the details of a trade secret worth $100,000 to other firms. Clearly, the worker cannot pay for the training, even though the skill involved is general, in the sense that it is valuable to other firms. When such training is involved, the firm providing the training needs another way to protect itself. The best way relies on a contractual mechanism, the "covenant not to compete." This is an explicit clause in a labor contract limiting the postemployment options of the worker and forbidding him from using certain skills, either for himself or for other employers.

There are some points that a manager should note regarding such covenants. First, they are not free. An employee will demand a higher wage if he is required to accept a contract with such a clause. Therefore, an employer should be careful only to specify such covenants where there really are assets to protect—trade secrets and customer lists (those expensive to develop). It is generally not worth obtaining agreement on such a clause merely to try to reduce potential postemployment competition from workers.*

Second, it is important to distinguish between "normal" general training, which the employee can pay for (by accepting reduced wages during training, for example) and that sort of general training which is worth protecting. Generally the latter will be too valuable for the employee to pay for. It is not worth having the employee sign a covenant if all he will be taught are normal, widely available skills such as welding.

Third, as an employee, a manager should be aware of these distinctions. If an employer requests that a manager sign such a contract, the manager should be sure that his compensation is adjusted accordingly. Moreover, a manager should determine what sort of training is involved. If it is normal general training, a manager might try to dissuade the employer from requiring such a contract.

Team Production

A third reason for organizing work within a firm rather then relying on outside contracting is that some tasks are the output of a *team*. A simple example is two men lifting cargo. In such a task, total output is a function of the inputs of both workers. It is not possible to measure the output of each. A monitor of some sort is needed to ensure that neither engages in shirking. This combination—a monitor and more than one worker—is already a firm, in the sense that with even this simple set of inputs it is no longer possible to rely on the market for policing. Rather, some central direction is involved.

Most employment situations are obviously vastly more complicated. The complications can often be reduced to combinations of team production and specialized resources. In fact, some of the specialized resources are those associated with human capital acquired while working with other members of a team.

Where much of the firm's output is produced by specialized labor working in teams, labor contracts become complex. The key goal of the firm in this situation is to provide incentives for workers to acquire the

* Moreover, in general, the courts are much more likely to enforce the clause if it is used to protect valuable information than if it is used to reduce competition.

very specific human capital for working with the team, and to avoid having productive members of the team quit, because this will reduce the value of other members of the team.

In this circumstance, it is worthwhile for the firm to make various commitments to the workforce in order to prove that it will not attempt to exploit any quasirents from the workers. Such commitments include substantial job security and agreements to arbitrate any employee termination. Additionally, workplaces with these characteristics commonly rely on "internal labor markets," a system in which most promotions are from within. All of these devices, commonly associated with labor unions, are in the interest of the firm in situations where there are specialized skills and team production.

An additional problem is created in the context of team production. If there is shirking, it is by definition impossible to determine which team member is responsible. As a result, efficient contracts must reward or penalize the entire team. However, for such contracts to work, they must have discontinuities. An example of such a contract is one in which a bonus is paid to all workers if productivity goals are exceeded. This creates a discontinuity at the desired level. Another example is a decision to fire all members of a team if productivity is below a set level. Such schemes will not work in partnerships, which explains why most firms (except in certain specialized situations, such as those applying to law firms, discussed in Chapter 4) are organized as traditional firms with ownership and labor separated.

BONDING

Workers with specific training which has been paid for by the employer are in a position to appropriate for themselves the quasirents associated with this training. It is in the interests of both the employee and the firm to avoid such exploitation. The employer of course does not want to be held up. The worker would like to be in a position to be able to prove that he will not exploit the firm because the firm is then more likely to invest in providing training for the worker. In other words, both the employee and the employer would like to devise a method by which the employee can *bond* himself not to exploit any quasirents. This bonding is analogous to the creation of a hostage, as discussed above.

Because a worker with human capital specific to a firm is worth more to this firm than to any other, the firm will pay him something more than his alternative wage. This additional payment serves two functions. First, it gives the employee an incentive to remain with the firm so that the firm can recoup its human capital investment. If the employee leaves this firm, he will not be paid anything for his specific human capital since this capital is worthless (by definition) to any other employer.

Second, this payment above alternatives can serve to protect the firm by acting as a bond. The worker receives a premium for working in this firm. However, he is not receiving the full value of his specialized human capital, since the firm paid for the acquisition of this capital. The worker may therefore try to appropriate the quasirent associated with the human capital by demanding a higher wage. However, if the firm does not accede in this demand and instead fires the worker, the worker will lose the share of the earnings on his specialized capital which he would otherwise have earned over his period of employment. Therefore, this premium over the value of the worker's market value is a bond which reduces or eliminates the incentive of the worker to hold up the employer. The employer also loses if he fires the worker. However, for the employer, his reputation is involved. If it becomes known that an employer will fire workers who attempt to appropriate the value of specialized human capital, then other workers will not attempt such appropriation.

An example of the loss of such a bond was the 1981 strike of air traffic controllers, employees of the U.S. government. These workers had human capital in air traffic control. Because the government runs all U.S. airports, this capital was valuable only to the government, and therefore was specific. The controllers went on strike in an attempt to appropriate for themselves the value of this capital. All strikers were fired and not rehired, and apparently most or all afterwards earned considerably less than their wage as air traffic controllers. The government did undertake some additional expenses in training a new air traffic control staff. However, there have since been no strikes against the government. In particular, when the air traffic controllers struck, there was also talk of a postal strike, but this never materialized.

In fact, bonding of this sort can be used in many situations where there is a possibility of employee shirking or opportunism. Bonding is especially important where the worker is in a position of trust and the employer wants to prevent cheating. Consider the following payment scheme: (1) The worker posts a bond with the firm. (2) During the term of employment the worker earns more than his opportunity cost. The additional earnings are approximately equal to the interest on the bond.

(3) Upon retirement the worker receives back as a pension or a lump sum payment the value of the bond. If the worker is detected cheating during employment, the bond is forfeit.

Such schemes have certain desirable properties. First, the worker over the course of employment is paid no more than his opportunity cost. Each year, payments are higher than in alternative employment, but only by the amount of the interest on the bond. Second, there are strong incentives against cheating or shirking because such shirking, if detected, will involve loss of the bond. Moreover, the up-front payment by the worker need not be in cash. Rather, it can be in the form of a reduced salary for a specified period of time. If the worker accepts a salary below alternatives during training, for example, this would create exactly the sort of bond involved here. The return of the bond will often be in the form of a larger pension than the worker would otherwise receive.

Such payment schemes should be seriously considered in jobs where there is a potential for shirking. The greater the possibility of shirking, the greater the advantage of such employment methods. Such techniques are particularly valuable where the worker is in a position to exploit more than the value of his own human capital from the firm, i.e., in a position to receive bribes. For these workers, we often observe that relatively early retirement with large pensions are a significant part of compensation, and the fear of loss of the pension will often serve to eliminate shirking.

A variant is simply to increase the worker's wage over the course of his working life, with earnings being below productivity when the worker is young and higher than productivity when the worker is older. Thus, the bond is in the form of expected higher earnings as the worker ages, which will be lost if the worker quits or shirks and is fired. One implication of this scheme is that workers will continue to work beyond the time that employers want them to work, since at some age workers will be earning more than their value, measured in terms of productivity. This tension has been suggested as an explanation for mandatory retirement in firms.

If a worker has a sufficiently sensitive position, it may be worthwhile overpaying him even if he cannot post a bond. The overpayment would be in the form of a higher salary rather than in alternative employment and a generous pension. Such overpayments will have costs to the firm, but it may well be that these extra costs are less than the expected cost to the firm of cheating by the employee.

The use of this type of payment scheme will often mean that workers, and particularly senior managers, will have reasonable expectations of future bonuses or other forms of deferred compensation. Such future bonuses may also be methods of rewarding managers who turn out to be more productive than average. In these circumstances, even though there may be no contracts, it will sometimes be the case that managers will expect to receive future payments. The payments cannot be contractual because part of the payment is for extra productivity which is revealed only after the employee is hired, and these payments cannot be contracted for at the time of hiring when actual productivity is uncertain. We will discuss such payments below in the section on takeovers.

If the worker posts a bond or has other reasons for expecting future compensation, then the firm is in a position to hold up the employee and exploit the value of the bond by falsely accusing the worker of shirking and firing him. However, this incentive is limited. This sort of opportunism should be less of a problem for a firm than for a worker, since a firm has a reputation. The board of directors, representing the firm, will have an incentive to pay such expected compensation because it will preserve the ability of the firm to hire high-quality managers. If the board behaves opportunistically and does not pay these bonuses where they are reasonably expected, the ability of the firm to hire managers will be reduced and managers will not be willing to post bonds. The effect of reputation should be particularly strong in the market for managers since they can be expected to communicate with each other and indicate that their expectations were not honored. However, for a new firm there will be no reputation, and therefore the firm may have to forego bonds from its employees until its reputation becomes established. Alternatively, or additionally, the firm may want to agree to arbitration of employee firings in order to prove that it will not behave opportunistically.

One interesting example of a bonding mechanism involving labor unions is an underfunded pension plan. Unions are common in manufacturing industries where there is a substantial amount of fixed, or sunk, capital, which creates large quasirents. Workers can then engage in holdup and exploit these quasirents. A union which controls the firm's access to labor is in a position to extract these quasirents from stockholders, and conceivably to drive the firm into bankruptcy. (One theory of optimal union behavior is that the union should set a time path of wages so that the firm goes bankrupt on the day the last original union member retires.) However, if the workers depend on the firm for pensions and if the pension fund is underfunded, then bankruptcy would deprive the workers of this asset. The pension liabilities serve as a "hostage" and constrain the union from appropriating the firm's quasi-rents. Underfunded pension plans are most common in industries with powerful unions and large sunk costs.

The existence of payment schemes which pay more than worker productivity means that at any time there may be additional workers who want jobs at the firm. Therefore, the firm might be able to hire these workers at lower wages than it is now paying. Nonetheless, even though there is excess supply of labor of this sort at the going wage, it is not in the firm's interests to reduce wages. If workers are hired at reduced wages, the benefits of bonds created by the excess payments will be lost.

There is another disadvantage of lowering wages. Workers may self-select in terms of quality based on wages, so that only lower quality workers will offer themselves to the firm at lower wages. This provides an additional incentive to refrain from lowering wages. We see below that similar considerations can operate in capital markets and in product markets.

CONTESTS

Consider the following situation: There are several workers with similar jobs. For all workers, output depends both on the effort of the worker and on some external condition which is difficult to observe, such as general economic conditions in the relevant area, which has a common effect on all workers. If conditions are bad, all workers will do relatively worse than if conditions are good, but the performance of any given worker depends on her effort.

In this case, a *contest* may serve as the best method of rewarding workers. This contest will take the form of rewarding the most productive worker with some prize. The prize may be cash, or some real good. In either case, the focus is on the worker's relative, not absolute, productivity. This is because using relative productivity enables the firm to separate out the effect of external conditions and the effort put forth by the employee, and implicitly reward effort. Such compensation schemes are common with salesmen, where the most productive salesman may be given a bonus, or a free vacation, or some other payment. Schemes like this can also be used with promotion as the reward. If there are several managers competing for a promotion, then the most productive may be awarded the job.

However, there is one modification which will sometimes be useful if promotions are used as contest rewards. If it is important to motivate the contestants for the promotion, it may be worthwhile to pay a higher salary to the winner than the job itself would demand. For example, if we are trying to motivate salesmen and the reward is a promotion to sales manager, then this job might carry a premium over and above its productivity. This is because the premium associated with being sales manager will serve not only to pay and motivate the sales manager himself, but also to motivate salesmen to try harder to become sales manager. (As a boy, I sold encyclopedias door-to-door, and was impressed with the fact that all of the sales managers, who were promoted salesmen, drove Cadillacs. This was clearly a device aimed at motivating salesmen, not at motivating the sales manager himself, who probably would have preferred more cash. Cash, however, would not have been as good a motivator for lower level employees because it is more difficult to observe cash than a Cadillac.)

An important type of contest is an "elimination career ladder." Begin with a large number of entry-level employees. These compete, with some dropping out at each stage. The ultimate reward is promotion to the very top position. However, note that as an employee advances through the hierarchy, the number of potential future promotions, and hence the rewards for hard work, are reduced. This is potentially costly because those managers who have progressed relatively far in the hierarchy are more productive, and also they are at each stage in charge of increasing amounts of the firm's resources. It is therefore important to motivate these successful, powerful managers to provide maximum efforts. In order to provide this motivation, the very top rewards in such contests must be much larger than would otherwise be the case.

One advantage of a contest over a piece-rate scheme is that the contest does not impose the same level of risk on workers as does a piece-rate payment scheme, but can still provide substantial incentives. This is because with a contest even workers with relatively low productivity still receive their normal earnings, but no "bonus." Therefore, such schemes might be considered in situations where current rewards are heavily based on piece-rate payment schedules. Since piece schedules impose risk on workers for which they demand compensation, there might be a possibility of savings in total wage costs by using a less risky scheme.

There are, however, limits to the use of contests. First, top managers control the overall performance of the firm. Since contests reward only relative performance, there is little incentive for a manager to worry about absolute performance. If the entire firm goes bankrupt division by division, then the manager of the last division left will be rewarded because he has done better than other managers. Top managers can control the absolute level of performance of the firm by mechanisms such as investment strategies. Therefore, rewards determined by contests, which are related to relative performance, are limited for such managers. An alternative is to use a measure based on performance of other firms within the same industry; as seen in the next chapter, the market may informally make use of this device already.

Second, contests create incentives for managers to attempt to harm others so as to come out ahead themselves, an example of the kind of influence activities discussed above. This can be costly to the firm in some circumstances. In cases where there are possibilities for cooperation among managers, and where such cooperation is productive for the firm, the possibility of using contests is limited. For one example, when divisions are profit centers which deal with each other through internal transactions, as discussed above in Chapter 2, transactions between divisions are difficult if both managers are seeking the same promotion. For another example, contests may be useful for motivating outside salesmen who do not interact with each other or with each other's customers. They are less useful for salesmen in a store, for a contest would give one salesman an incentive to discourage customers of another salesman from making a purchase.

HIERARCHIES

Workforces are organized as hierarchies. At the top is the president or CEO, reporting to the board of directors. There are then several levels of managers, and ultimately the actual production workers supervised by the lowest level of management. An important issue is the design of the wage structure within this hierarchy.

There are several factors which determine the rate of increase of wages within the hierarchy. First, as mentioned above, part of the function of a promotion is to serve as a reward in a contest, and such rewards must be valuable. For firms which rely more heavily on such contests, wages should increase more quickly. Second, as managers move up the hierarchy they become more productive. This is for two reasons: (1) managers controlling more resources are able to have more impact on the profits of the firm; higher level jobs are more productive. And (2) it generally pays to assign more able managers to higher levels because they do control more resources, so that higher level managers are more productive and able individuals. Therefore, wages should increase more quickly in the hierarchy as the amount of responsibility increases, and as the additional ability needed by higher level managers increases. The final reason for increasing pay is that promotions serve as a signal of the productivity of a manager to outside observers, precisely because more productive individuals are more likely to be promoted. Outsiders have difficulty in determining the productivity of a manager in a job within a firm. However, when a manager is promoted this is a sign to outsiders that she is a productive manager, and worth more. Outsiders are therefore likely to attempt to hire away promoted managers, and increased wages are useful to prevent this from occurring. When the market for managers in an industry is more competitive, there should be a greater increase in wages within the hierarchy.

OUTSIDE AGENTS

Sometimes it will be necessary to hire outside agents to perform complex tasks. These hired parties may actually be called agents, as in real estate agents; or they may be called consultants. Outside attorneys are another example of hired outsiders. In general, it will pay to hire such outsiders in situations where the firm needs some specialized skill on an interim basis, or where economies of scale or economics of scope are such that it does not pay to hire some type of input on a permanent basis. For example, firms will occasionally need highly specialized legal skills (as when litigation is pending) but not on a sufficient basis to justify retaining enough skilled attorneys on a permanent basis. Where possible, such agents should be paid on a piece-rate basis (as our initial example of messenger firms) but this is not possible if the job is sufficiently complex.

The theory of ownership discussed in the last chapter is relevant here as well. When a job is done by an employee, the firm itself retains residual rights in that it can specify what tasks the employee will do. When it is done by an outside contractor, although the contract will generally be very specific, residual rights remain with the contractor who has the right to do any action which is not specified in the contract in any way he chooses. Outside agents should therefore be used in situations in which it is too costly for the firm to specify the exact methods of performing some task. These will be situations in which the firm has only sporadic need of the particular skill at issue.

When outside agents are used, agency problems of the sort discussed in this chapter exist. Consider, for a simple example, a real estate agent. Normally, such agents are paid on a fixed rate commission, such as 6 or 7 percent. This means that for each $1,000 additional price that the agent gets for an asset, he gains only $60. As a result, the agent gains less from increasing the selling price of the property than does the principal. This creates an incentive for the agent to urge the seller to sell at a price below the optimum. It is important to be aware of this problem and take into account the differing incentives of the parties to the transaction in making decisions based on agents' recommendations. A real estate agent, for example, may advise a seller to accept an offer when it might be in the interest of the seller to wait for a better offer.

It is possible to structure contracts to reduce this problem. The sort of contracts discussed above, called two-part tariffs, are useful in this context. For example, assume that the best estimate of the value of a property is $100,000, but there is a 50 percent chance that the property will sell for $110,000. Assume also that a real estate agent normally gets 6 percent commission. Then a contract giving 5 percent on the first $100,000 and 20 percent on everything over this would give the agent greater incentives to maximize the value of the property. This contract would have at least the same expected value to the agent as the original 6 percent contract, and a greater value to the principal, and so might be efficient. Such contracts are common in complex sales situations. The contract appears to increase the risk borne by the agent. However, since an agent will sign many such contracts, over all the variance of his expected income may not increase substantially, and the wealth-creating aspects of the contract could easily outweigh the slight increase in risk.

There are also agency problems associated with hiring an attorney. Contracts are often structured to minimize these problems, but they cannot be eliminated. For example, in many types of cases, plaintiff's attorneys are paid on a contingency basis, and the payment is in terms of a fraction (often one-third) of the settlement. Such a contract gives the attorney an incentive to come close to maximizing the award, since the attorney gets a substantial fraction of the amount. Nonetheless, the attorney might have too strong an incentive to settle a case since almost the entire cost of litigation is borne by the attorney and he only gains one-third of the returns. Sometimes contingent contracts are written with a higher return to the attorney if litigation occurs.

Defendants and others, often large firms, commonly pay their attorneys by the hour. This creates other incentive problems, in that the attorney might spend too much time on the case. One possible solution is internal monitoring, as by the general counsel. Such monitoring will not be perfect, but it will serve as a partial check on agency problems. In such situations, the reputation of the attorney is also an important control, and it may often pay to spend relatively more on attorneys in order to hire a firm with a substantial reputation and reduce incentives for shirking.

Firms will often have ongoing need for attorneys. A natural question is the extent to which attorneys should be employees of the firm (the general counsel) and the extent to which they should be retained as outside counsel. One issue is economies of scale: A firm may not have need of full-time attorneys. In this case, outside counsel will be cheapest. However, if a firm does have need for one or more full-time attorneys, then the principles discussed in the last chapter become relevant. To the extent that lawyers for the firm have invested substantial amounts in specific knowledge with respect to the company itself, then this investment may make the firm subject to opportunistic behavior on the part of the attorneys. The reputation of the law firm can reduce the chances for such holdup, but, as we will see in Chapter 5, particular attorneys within law firms can shirk by leaving the law firm, so that there is always a chance for holdup. Therefore, to the extent feasible (depending on workload), a firm should rely on inside counsel for firm-specific knowledge.

SUMMARY

The goals of workers and firms are not identical. This can lead to agency costs, which are essentially the labor market's version of the costs of opportunism and shirking. A useful starting point is to observe that if the firm relied entirely on contract labor paid on a piecework basis, there would be no agency costs. Therefore, we ask why the firm will not use this method of compensation.

The answer is found in three parts. First, workers are risk averse and prefer employment relations which do not place the entire risk of a bad outcome on them. Second, workers acquire specialized skills, specialized to the firm, and the existence of these skills means that certain complex contracts are useful. Third, much output is produced by teams, and a team is by definition a primitive firm. Situations involving both specialized training and team production are especially interesting and important.

Discussion of employment relations in these terms provides many useful insights for management of labor. It is possible to devise complex, two-part compensation contracts which can motivate labor better than normal contracts, and still save on costs. These contracts can improve productivity or reduce costs, for example, by creating more efficient mechanisms for risk sharing. We can determine the best form for "covenants not to compete" in labor contracts. In the discussion of bonding, several devices were proposed for avoiding appropriation on both sides of the labor market, and we indicated that there may be disadvantages from offering lower wages, even if workers could be hired at these wages. We discussed the use of contest-like devices for rewarding managers under certain conditions. We were also able to devise principles for indicating the rate which wages should increase as workers move up a job hierarchy. Wages should increase more quickly within a firm as the firm relies more heavily on contests to motivate managers, as productivity increases within the hierarchy, and as competition for talented managers from other firms increases.

In hiring outside workers, such as real estate agents or attorneys, there are often agency problems created. It is possible to design contracts to minimize these problems; such contracts are often two-part payment schedules. It is also possible to use monitoring, as by the firm's general counsel. Reputation, as always, is also important in these situations. Nonetheless, managers should be aware of the remaining incentive problems in making decisions when agents are involved. One implication is that firms should rely on inside counsel for tasks requiring firm-specific knowledge whenever economies of scale make this feasible.

REFERENCES

Alchian, Armen, and Demsetz, Harold. "Production, Information Costs, and Economic Organization." *American Economic Review* 62 (1972):777. Reprinted in *The Economic Nature of the Firm,* edited by Louis Putterman.

Arrow, Kenneth J. "The Economics of Agency." In *Principles and Agents,* edited by John W. Pratt and Richard J. Zeckhauser.

Becker, Gary S., and Stigler, George J. "Law Enforcement, Malfeasance, and Compensation of Enforcers." *Journal of Legal Studies* 3 (1974):1.

Epstein, Richard A. "Agency Costs, Employment Contracts, and Labor Unions." In *Principles and Agents,* edited by John W. Pratt and Richard J. Zeckhauser.

Holmstrom, Bengt R. "Moral Hazard in Teams." *The Bell Journal of Economics* 13 (1982):324.

Holmstrom, Bengt R., and Tirole, Jean. "The Theory of the Firm." In *Handbook of Industrial Organization.* edited by Richard Schmalensee and Robert Willig.

Ippolito, Richard. "The Economic Function of Underfunded Pension Plans." *Journal of Law and Economics* 28 (1985):611.

Lazear, Edward P. "Why Is There Mandatory Retirement?" *Journal of Political Economy* 87 (1979):1261.

Lazear, Edward P., and Rosen, Sherwin. "Rank-Order Tournaments and Optimum Labor Contracts." *Journal of Political Economy* 89 (1981):841.

Milgrom, Paul R. "Employment Contracts, Influence Activities, and Efficient Organization Design." *Journal of Political Economy* 96 (1988):42.

Rosen, Sherwin. "Prizes and Incentives in Elimination Tournaments." *American Economic Review* 76 (1986):701.

Rubin, Paul H., and Shedd, Peter. "Human Capital and Covenants Not to Compete." *Journal of Legal Studies* 10 (1981). Reprinted in *Business Firms and the Common Law,* edited by Paul Rubin.

Stiglitz, Joseph E. "The Causes and Consequences of the Dependence of Quality on Price." *Journal of Economic Literature* 25 (1987):1.

Williamson, Oliver E. *The Economic Institutions of Capitalism.* chapters 9–10. New York: Free Press, 1985.

PART II
Capital and Finance

$-4-$

Some Notes on Finance

To understand finance, it is useful conceptually to start with an individual establishing a small firm—a sole proprietorship—using only his own capital. In such an enterprise, there are no agency costs because the owner (and sole decision maker) bears the costs of all decisions, and reaps the gains from any decisions. As long as he has sufficient capital, the proprietor will make any investments whose risk-adjusted expected return is positive. The owner is therefore the *residual claimant*, the party who has rights to any returns earned by the enterprise after all contractual payments are made. Residual claimants are therefore also residual risk bearers, since they are responsible for any losses suffered by the enterprise.

But what happens if the owner runs out of money when a profitable investment comes along? It is at this point that financial issues become relevant. The owner must now raise money from some source in order to finance this profitable venture. The alternatives are debt or equity.

If the owner turns to the stock (equity) market, then the stockholders become the primary residual claimants. In smaller firms, the owner may play this role. Partners are residual claimants in firms organized as partnerships, such as law firms. The significance of the residual claimant is crucial in understanding principles of finance, and of firm structure in general.

If the manager of a firm were the residual claimant, as is true in some small firms, then there would be no problem of shirking and no agency costs. The owner-manager would make all decisions correctly, in that he would bear any costs of incorrect decisions. For example, such a person would take time off from work if, and only if, the value to him of the additional leisure were greater than the sacrificed profits. An owner-manager would invest in all projects which he expected to at least cover their cost of capital, and in no other projects. There would be no incentive for unwarranted leisure in such a firm, and no incentive for any other excessive shirking.

Few real firms, and no large ones, are run in this way. Large firms are run as corporations with the following relevant properties: (1) The residual claimant is a large mass of diffuse stockholders, few of whom have any direct interest in running or monitoring the firm; the return to stockholders is risky and related to the earnings of the firm; stockholders have ultimate control over the firm. (2) Additionally, there are bondholders who lend money to the firm for a fixed return; the returns to bondholders are much less risky than the returns to stockholders. (3) There is a board of directors which performs some monitoring functions on behalf of stockholders with respect to top managers. (4) There are outside auditors who also monitor the behavior of top managers. And (5), notwithstanding (3) and (4), top managers seem to have substantial discretion in operating the firm. This discretion has often been called the "separation of ownership and control." (An intermediate case between the single proprietorship and the large corporation is the closely held corporation, discussed below.)

There are two reasons for such separation. First, many persons with the tastes and ability to be top managers lack the capital to finance the firm in its entirety. Therefore, it is efficient to devise ways for potential managers to have access to capital, even if they do not themselves own it. Second, even if a manager does own enough capital to establish a firm, general principles of risk aversion indicate that the manager would prefer not to risk all of his own capital in the enterprise. Or, what is the same thing, the required compensation for the manager would be less if he did not need to risk all of his capital in the firm because he would not need to be paid as much of a risk premium.

The cost of the separation is the creation of incentives for some degree of shirking or opportunistic behavior. The assets of the firm will not earn as much as they would if there were no separation of ownership and control. Thus, in seeking to devise efficient structures for the capital of a firm, we must consider the interrelations between three factors: access to capital, risk spreading, and shirking. It is also important to note that we cannot study finance in a vacuum. The financial structure of the firm is closely and intimately related to its organizational structure.

As a manager, your goal is to raise capital at as low a cost as possible, and to raise that amount of capital for which the marginal cost of additional capital equals the marginal return from additional investing.

As always, you should read this chapter with two purposes in mind. First, you should look for incentives you can offer to providers of capital in order to encourage investment in the firm. An important part of these incentives will be ways of risk spreading. Second, you should look for ways in which you can credibly commit yourself and other managers in the firm not to engage in shirking (in any of its myriad forms) in order to credibly promise as high a return as feasible to the sources of capital. Lenders and investors will understand possibilities of shirking, and to the extent that shirking cannot be eliminated, costs will be higher and profits less, so less will be invested in the firm. To the extent that shirking can be reduced, profits will increase because of reduced costs, more will be invested, and more potential investments in projects will cover their costs of capital. Consequently, the firm will be larger.

Note that simply offering a higher interest rate will often not be an efficient way of generating additional lending for the firm. In the last chapter, we indicated that it might be in the firm's interest to pay more than necessary for labor because lower wage labor might also be of lower quality. The same principle applies to lenders: Borrowers willing to offer high-interest rates reveal themselves to be self-selected as poor risks or else they would have been able to borrow at a lower rate elsewhere. Therefore, there are limits to your ability to increase your line of credit by offering a higher payment. Other methods of bonding or guaranteeing repayment might be more efficient than offering higher interest rates.

DEBT

The payments for debt (interest on bank loans or bonds) are fixed and independent of the profitability of the firm. This is one major advantage of debt (the other is the tax deductibility of interest payments on debt). Since payments are fixed, they do not affect the residual, and the proprietor remains the residual claimant for all of the profits or losses of the firm. There is no incentive created for shirking because debt does not affect the size of the residual. This is a key benefit from debt financing.

But there is a cost as well. The cost is associated with the possibility of bankruptcy for the firm. If the firm goes bankrupt, then the owner will lose his equity, and bondholders will also lose the value of their investments. But there is an asymmetry between owners and lenders. Consider some potential risky major investment facing the firm. If it is successful, the firm will earn substantial returns. If it fails, the firm will go bankrupt. Bondholders will suffer if the firm declares bankruptcy, but they will not gain if the venture is successful since their returns are contractually fixed and independent of the success of the project. The owner will reap the entire gains if the venture is successful, but will lose only his own share of the value of the firm if it is unsuccessful.

This asymmetry creates an incentive for opportunistic behavior on the part of the owner-manager of the firm. As the share of the firm's capital financed by debt increases, this incentive for opportunism also increases because the owner has relatively less to lose from failure. (This is the underlying cause of the current savings and loan crisis, discussed in detail below: Owners risked mostly capital of depositors when they made risky investments. Of course, depositors did not care either, since the government insured their losses.) Bondholders and other creditors are generally aware of this incentive (unless they are a governmental body). As a result, as the firm becomes relatively more indebted (more leveraged) the payment demanded for lending money to the firm will increase to adjust for this increased risk. Some large creditors of the firm may also engage directly in monitoring the firm to make sure that it does not engage in overly risky behavior. Such lenders, discussed in the next chapter, will be called *active investors*.

Ultimately, however, the firm may turn to the other form of capital, equity. At which point this will be done depends on several factors which determine the risk associated with debt. One factor is the nature of the industry. If the industry under consideration is one which can be monitored relatively easily, such as a utility, the possibilities for excessive risk taking are limited. For utilities, monitoring is relatively easy since the sort of activities undertaken by utilities are well known and easily measured. Thus, for business which can be monitored, debt can be used relatively more easily than for businesses (for example, research labs) which engage in risky and unusual activities, and which cannot be easily monitored. (An industry in which managers can exploit investors because monitoring is difficult will be called *plastic*.) For such industries, an important part of creditor behavior is monitoring of the activities of the firm. Some types of monitoring can be done by outside agents, such as auditing firms. Therefore, managers in industries where it is relatively easy for outside agents to monitor activities should rely on debt and offer lenders a promise of substantial outside monitoring. On the other hand, managers in relatively more plastic industries will rely less on debt.

The importance of this set of contracts can best be seen in an industry where the requirements were violated. The U.S. government insures deposits in the savings and loan industry. This insurance means that creditors (individual depositors) have no incentive to monitor the soundness of their investments since the insurer, an agency of the government, will pay them if the S & L goes under. The insurer is the residual claimant. Traditionally, insurers have relied on intensive direct monitoring of lending activity because they are liable in the event of failure. (In banking, the bank examiners perform this function.) In the early 1980s, however, policies changed. The government maintained its role as insurer but greatly reduced its monitoring of the industry. As a result, owners of savings and loans made excessively risky loans, precipitating the current crisis. Private insurers would not have allowed themselves to be put into this position because of the associated risks of opportunism, which did indeed catch up with the government (and, ultimately, with taxpayers who are the ultimate insurers).

Another factor which is relevant for possibilities of using debt is the sort of capital involved in a particular expansion. One possibility available to creditors is to seize the actual assets which are collateral for their loans. This option becomes more viable as the capital involved is more marketable. As capital becomes more specialized to the firm, its value to creditors falls. On the other hand, as capital is more general and less specialized, it becomes more valuable to creditors. For example, a truck is general capital, valuable to many firms and obviously mobile, and therefore is useful as collateral for a loan. On the other hand, a special-purpose machine designed for use in a particular factory is specialized and would be virtually worthless on its own to a creditor, so this type of capital cannot serve as collateral. Creditors would be more willing to make loans backed up by general capital than by special capital. (Or, equivalently, creditors would demand lower interest for loans backed by general than by specific capital.) As a manager, if you are raising money to finance the acquisition of relatively mobile, nonappropriable capital, you should consider the possibility of special-purpose dedicated bonds for financing this acquisition.

Note the parallel between this observation and the possibility of appropriating quasirents from capital, discussed in Chapter 1. As the returns from capital become more easily appropriated, the capital becomes less suited as collateral for a loan. Capital whose returns cannot be appropriated is less specialized, and more suited to serve as collateral. The core activities of a firm, involving specialized assets, will be financed by equity; peripheral activities, involving unspecialized capital, can be financed through debt. If the capital of a firm is primarily unspecialized, the firm should rely most heavily on debt. If such a firm acquires too much equity relative to debt, its financial structure is out of equilibrium and there are profitable opportunities for realignment, discussed in the next chapter.

An extreme form of debt finance, which shows the nature of the tradeoffs, is leasing. When capital equipment is leased, the lessor finances the capital in its entirety, and the firm using the capital pays only the rental cost. Leasing therefore takes advantage of the market as a determinant of price, and is desirable when it is possible. Clearly, however, leasing is feasible only in a limited set of circumstances. First, the capital must be mobile and redeployable; no firm would lease specialized machines used in a factory because this would create appropriable quasirents and the leasing firm would expect to be exploited. Leasing is also only possible when the owner can either perform or easily monitor maintenance, since the firm leasing the equipment would have no incentive to perform the efficient level of maintenance. However, where these conditions are met, leasing does illustrate the possibility of extreme debt financing and, when feasible, should be seriously considered.

Payments to service debt (interest and repayment of principal) require that managers pay out earnings to bondholders, which serves a useful purpose. There is always an agency problem between managers and residual claimants. One form it takes is the desire of managers to invest in ways which are not wealth maximizing. For example, managers might prefer to use earnings for growth rather than paying earnings out to stockholders, even if the firm is growing in nonmaximizing directions. If managers are contractually forced to pay out earnings as debt service, there is less possibility of retaining such earnings for nonmaximizing purposes. In other words, debt, with its forced payments schedule, serves as a bond. Since dividends on stock are not contractual, they cannot serve the same function.

One interesting and controversial form of debt is the so called "junk" bond. These are simply bonds with relatively high risk which pay correspondingly high yields. In one sense, they may be viewed as marketable commercial loans. There are various controversies associated with this form of finance, often with respect to their use in takeovers. However, it is important to note that in general junk bonds are merely another form of debt finance, particularly useful for smaller, newer, or riskier firms. Managers of such firms should use this form of debt whenever it is cheaper than alternatives (such as commercial borrowing or equity finance). Lenders who lend through junk bonds will generally investigate the firm carefully and take an active role in monitoring the firm, so that the association of risk and the offer of a higher return, discussed above, will be minimized.

EQUITY

There are several reasons why a firm might rely on equity. First, the firm might desire to raise additional capital and the marginal costs of equity might be less than those of debt. As the amount of debt used by a firm increases, the incentives for overly risky investments also increase because the owner-manager has relatively less to lose from bankruptcy. As risk increases, lenders require proportionally higher returns. Therefore, the marginal cost of raising money through debt increases as the fraction of the value of the firm financed by debt increases. Second, an owner of a firm might want to convert his ownership interests into cash, and selling of part of the firm might be the most efficient way to achieve this goal. Finally, as firms become larger, agency problems between various managers become more significant because it becomes more difficult for the peak manager to control the firm. At some point, these problems and the associated costs may be sufficiently large so that there is little if any additional cost from creating stock and accepting the associated control loss and agency costs.

The disadvantage of outside equity is that it dilutes the correspondence between the profits of the firm and the profits of the decision maker. This creates substantial agency costs. Decision makers may begin to engage in various forms of shirking because some or all of the costs of shirking are borne by stockholders. Since the manager no longer receives all of the profits of the firm, she no longer bears all of the costs associated with reduced profits. This means that managers may allow costs, including costs associated with inefficient, on-the-job consumption, to increase.

Inefficient, on-the-job consumption is that share of such consumption which costs more than its value to workers. Workers would pay something for more pleasant working conditions, but agency costs may lead to excessive consumption, relative to its value. For example, managers may schedule sales meetings in Hawaii when a meeting in St. Louis (or no meeting at all) would be more cost effective from the perspective of the firm. The Hawaii meeting may cost $10,000 more than the St. Louis meeting, and the value to managers of the extra consumption may be only $4,000; it is in this sense that on-the-job consumption may be inefficient. (Of course, some owner-managers might also meet in Hawaii, so we cannot be sure that this form of consumption is inefficient.) Firms will spend some resources on monitoring this consumption, such as auditing expense accounts. However, it will not pay to reduce it to zero.

In the short run, managers benefit from such on-the-job consumption. However, earnings of managers will reflect this consumption and, since $1 of on-the-job consumption is generally worth less than $1, managers would prefer ways of reducing shirking and increasing compensation. It is for this reason that it is efficient for managers to attempt to bond themselves not to engage in such consumption. To the extent that such bonding is feasible and cost effective, there are possibilities for real gains to managers and to owners.

In addition to shirking by on-the-job consumption, managers may shirk by pursuing non-optimal investment policies. Such policies, which may involve not undertaking certain investments and undertaking certain others, may be much more costly to the firm than on-the-job consumption.

Managers may refrain from undertaking some profitable investments since, again, only part of the gain accrues to the decision maker. A manager has a substantial investment of human capital in the firm, and this creates a nondiversifiable, firm-specific risk. Managers may also have nondiversified equity interests in the firm because investors may require such investments in order to bond managers. Investors, on the other hand, can diversify their portfolios by investing in many companies.* Therefore, investors are less risk averse than managers with respect to potential bankruptcy of the firm.

This means that investors would like managers to undertake riskier investments than managers would like to undertake, as long as the investments have positive expected values. It also means that managers may undertake investments aimed at inefficiently expanding the size of the firm if such expansion reduces risk. (Note that this is the opposite of the problem created by debt finance, which leads to excessively risky investments by owner-managers.) In some circumstances, investors might want managers to liquidate the firm (if its asset value becomes greater than its going concern value) but managers would resist this strategy, since their human capital would then become much less

---

* Many economists think that the most efficient portfolio for investors is a mutual fund which mimics a broad equity index, such as Standard and Poor's.

valuable. As seen in the next chapter, this is one rationale behind a "golden parachute," a payment to managers in the event of certain types of takeovers.

Managers may also undertake some investments which are non-maximizing from the perspective of the firm if these investments provide benefits to the managers. One particularly important problem is the use of *free cash flow,* or cash flow over and above any which can be used to fund projects with positive present values when discounted at the relevant cost of capital. It is the quasirent stream associated with the going concern value of the firm. Such free cash flow should be returned to the shareholders if the value of the firm is to be maximized. However, managers will often have incentives to invest these funds in other activities, in part because of excessive managerial risk aversion created by nondiversified portfolios. For one extreme example, in the early 1980s oil companies were investing in drilling for oil when the value of $1.00 invested in this activity was only $.60. The use and misuse of free cash flow is important in understanding restructurings and takeovers, and is discussed in detail in the next chapter.

So far, the factors identified can explain the concentration of equity ownership of firms. The benefits of concentrated ownership are in terms of greater control and reduced shirking. The costs are in terms of increased risk associated with undiversified investments. Firms where greater concentration of ownership is more valuable will tend to have more concentrated ownership. Such firms will be in industries where monitoring of top management is valuable. As the environment in which the firm operates is more uncertain and variable (that is, as the environment is more plastic), there is more scope for managerial discretion, and therefore monitoring is more valuable. In such environments equity ownership will be more concentrated. Conversely, for regulated firms such as utilities, there is little scope for managerial shirking, and equity ownership should be less concentrated. (Utilities are a special case since they are monitored carefully by regulatory authorities, implying even less value of monitoring by owners than would be true for similar but nonregulated enterprises.) On the other hand, as a firm becomes larger, concentration of ownership requires greater undiversified investments and greater risk, so larger firms will have more diverse ownership.

In order to limit their potential losses from opportunism, equity owners demand and receive control over the firm. That is, equity owners become the residual claimants of the firm, and are able to determine its activities. They are also able to hire and fire other agents of the firm including the president or peak manager. In addition, because of the shirking problem created by the creation of equity, equity owners have devised various methods of direct monitoring to protect their positions. There are three major methods: outside auditing, control by the board of directors, and the market for corporate control. (The latter is discussed in the next chapter, dealing with takeovers.)

Outside auditors look for gross irregularities in management practice. As mentioned above, outside auditors perform functions which are valuable to bondholders as well as to stockholders. They are able to detect violations of trust in certain simple situations, but as possibilities for shirking become more subtle and as discretion of managers increases, the ability of auditors to detect shirking decreases. (For example, auditors can determine if a research scientist has overpaid for a piece of equipment, but they have a good deal of difficulty in determining if she is working on the most promising project from the firm's perspective, or on one which will enhance her own professional reputation. Auditors become less useful as activities become more plastic.)

The board of directors acts as the agent of the equity owners. In a large modern corporation, stock ownership is commonly diffuse, although the level of dispersion of equity ownership is determined by the factors identified above. Stockholders themselves will diversify their portfolios in order to spread risk among many investments, and thus reduce risk. As a result, no one stockholder will own a significant share of a firm, nor will a significant fraction of the wealth of any stockholder be invested in one firm. This means that stockholders have limited interest in monitoring the day-to-day activities of the firm. But stockholders do have an interest in having the firm run efficiently. Monitoring is delegated to the board of directors, the agents of the stockholders.

By and large, the board will not interfere in the day-to-day operations of the firm. However, it will have substantial power, such is the power to fire the management of the firm. This power clearly serves to limit the scope for opportunism on the part of management, though, because of information problems, there is still substantial room for some opportunistic behavior. There is evidence that replacement of the top management team by the board of directors is more common for firms which are underperforming relative to their industry. This evidence applies to the Fortune 500 companies, but it is probably true for smaller companies as well.

HYBRIDS AND CLOSELY HELD CORPORATIONS

So far, we have discussed debt and equity as if they were totally distinct, and stockholders and managers as if they were also distinct. In fact, in many cases there will be various hybrids. First, managers often have equity interests in firms, or contracts with payment based on profit. Even without these interests, managers have substantial amounts to lose from insolvency since they generally have specialized human capital and reputations invested in firms. Thus, the status of a manager is partially that of a residual claimant. Second, there are various forms of hybrid debt-equity instruments, such as preferred stock or convertible bonds. Some lenders or suppliers may take their returns as royalties rather than interest, again creating a hybrid status.

It is important to understand the principles of debt and equity and the costs and benefits of each. Once you understand these, then you can decide exactly which set of obligations and returns you want from each participant in an organization. An attorney can then structure the proper legal and financial instruments to achieve this mix. However, the desired mix is a business, not a legal, decision, and the role of the attorney is to structure the agreement which will accomplish what the manager wants. The attorney should not impose the terms of the agreement by establishing the legal structure.

One such intermediate case, between the single proprietorship and the large corporation, is the *closely held corporation*. This is a firm with a few stockholders, many of whom are also the top managers of the company. In two senses, this structure is intermediate between the other two. First, it has some of the features of each. Second, a successful single proprietorship may reorganize itself as a closely held corporation, and, if success continues, this firm may ultimately reorganize as a publicly traded corporation. (As we see in the next chapter, after a leveraged buyout a public firm may reorganize as a closely held corporation.) However, there are special agency problems associated with close corporations. You should understand these problems if you plan to structure your firm as such an enterprise, if you are considering taking a job with such a company, or if you are offered an opportunity to invest in such a company.

Consider an entrepreneur who has invested and prospered, and has reached the point where he has no funds of his own and needs additional financing in order to expand. For the reasons discussed above, he is unable to borrow additional funds (or the cost of borrowing has become prohibitive). One option is to try to raise money from a small number of investors. Some classes of potential investors are more likely to invest than others because they are in a favored position to avoid being victims of opportunism. One particularly attractive source of funds is family members, if they have the money. Another source is senior employees of the firm.

Shirking and opportunistic behavior is less likely between family members than between strangers because there are generally nonbusiness dealings between them. Therefore, opportunistic behavior will be less likely because someone who behaves opportunistically will not only alienate a business associate (whom he might not see again anyway) but will also alienate family members, and this could be more personally costly. There may even be genetic reasons for unwillingness to cheat relatives. (It is interesting that many business activities where there is no possibility of contractual enforcement, such as criminal enterprise, are organized along family lines.)

Another useful source of funds for such enterprises is borrowing from senior managers of the organization. Since these managers are already associated with the enterprise, they are in a position to monitor its behavior at low cost. Therefore, they would not anticipate being victims of opportunistic behavior, and could lend to the firm on more favorable terms than outsiders. If the firm is successful, these persons may have been paid substantial amounts in salaries, and may therefore have the capital to invest. It is also possible that suppliers or customers are in a position to make loans to a firm for growth purposes since they have some knowledge of the firm. However, since they are not as involved in day-to-day operations, monitoring by such lenders would be more costly than for insiders, and therefore terms would not be as favorable as from others.

In any of these cases, the firm has raised money from a particular class of investors. Commonly at this point the firm will be restructured as a corporation with the stock held by these investors. There will not be a market for the stock. There are several features of an efficient contract which can be explained in terms of the sorts of issues discussed above. In particular, note that financing of this firm is through "equity," but the equity has many of the characteristics of debt. The risk structure and incentive structure associated with this equity is intermediate between debt and publicly traded equity.

An alternative to organization as a close corporation is to seek finance through junk bonds, discussed above. Holders of junk bonds will often personally engage in monitoring of the firm, as will investors in close corporations. However, junk bond holders will not be insiders, so that their monitoring costs may be higher then similar costs of stockholders of close corporations and therefore the required return on junk bonds will be larger. If possible, it is probably preferable to organize as a close corporation if there are insiders with sufficient wealth to undertake the needed investment.

Since the stock is closely held, the owners do not gain the benefits of diversification of risk associated with stock in publicly traded companies. Since the owners are often managers, there is a double lack of diversification: Most of the wealth of the owners is invested in one corporation, and returns on both invested financial capital and on human capital are associated with this same entity, so that risk is again increased. Moreover, since there is no public market for the stock, an investment in a close corporation is much less liquid than an investment in a public company. This also means that it is more difficult to determine the value of the investment when a stock transaction does become desirable.

The main advantage of a close corporation is that there is little or no separation of ownership from management. Therefore, there is much less shirking of the sort discussed above. This can be a powerful advantage since shirking can be very costly. Additional advantages are the close control which can be maintained by the original owner and his close associates, and the savings in costs associated with public trading and regulation. Therefore, there are circumstances in which the advantages of a close corporation may be sufficiently valuable to outweigh this disadvantage to investors. If enough capital can be raised from close associates, then this form of enterprise is likely to be desirable. The agency problems associated with this organizational structure call for appropriate safeguards in contracts between the various owners.*

Since the owners of the equity have control over the company, and since they generally have a close role to play in management, there may be restrictions on alienability. That is, there may be limits on the transfer of shares since owners of shares, unlike the case in large corporations, have close day-to-day dealings with the corporation. A stockholder should not be able to sell the right to be company treasurer along with his shares without the approval of the president. This is the first sort of restriction which may be worthwhile.

* As in many other cases, the exact working out of these matters is complex and will require services of an attorney. However, as in other points in the book, it is important for managers to understand the issues with which the attorney will be concerned, and for the attorney to understand the underlying managerial issues.

Second, since shares are nonliquid, provisions must be made for transfer when this is necessary or worthwhile. If shares are owned by managers, there should be provisions for buying out these shares upon the death or retirement of the manager, or perhaps in case of an unresolvable conflict. If shares are owned by family members, there should be provisions for allowing them to liquidate without the shares going outside the family. A provision requiring the treasury to pay out retained earnings as dividends when there is a certain amount of cash in the treasury can keep this problem from becoming unmanageable by minimizing the amount of equity at issue. Otherwise, there should be provisions for establishing a transactions price (perhaps related to some easily observable value, such as sales) when a transaction becomes useful. There should also be provisions for forcing a transaction upon the occurrence of certain events.

Third, it is common for profits in closely held corporations to be paid out as salaries to the senior managers, who may also be the owners. However, this creates a potential shirking problem as those managers in control may pay themselves too much. One solution is to require large majority votes to approve salary payments. It may also be necessary to give investors contractual rights to jobs if these jobs are associated with past investments in the firm to be paid for through salaries.

As minority shareholders gain increased protection, the possibility of deadlock increases. Therefore, a fourth sort of provision is some method of resolving such disputes. One method is to require arbitration in the event of deadlock; another is to establish a third party who can vote to break a deadlock. However, if it is too easy to break a deadlock, incentives for good faith negotiation become weakened and deadlocks become more likely.

Close corporations are efficient structures for investments in one-time projects; for example, a real estate development business. Generally, a corporation is formed for each project and dissolved when the project is completed and sold. Here, large sums of liquid assets and large risks are involved. Moreover, assets are relatively plastic since the investment is in creation of a new entity, the project involved in the development. Creation of new entities is generally riskier and requires more major decisions than operating of an ongoing enterprise. For all of these reasons, close monitoring by investors is worthwhile because shirking is easy. This means that it will not pay for investors to invest small sums and forego monitoring due to the possibilities of shirking by managers. As a result, there will be relatively few relatively large investors in each project, a structure associated with a close corporation.

Finally, the corporation will be liquidated when the project is finished and sold, so that the problems of dividing up the assets will be simple. Each investor will own a specified share of the assets and when the project is sold, she will be paid her share.

In sum, a closely held corporation can overcome that set of agency problems associated with shirking because residual claimants are also managers. In this sense, a close corporation is similar to a single proprietorship. However, this will create an additional set of agency problems. These are associated with possibilities of expropriation of the investments of minority investors, and with the transfer of shares. Mechanisms have been suggested for minimizing but not eliminating these problems. It is not surprising that these tradeoffs exist; one message of this book is that nothing is free.

ORGANIZATIONAL STRUCTURE

So far, we have dealt with firms in which the most specialized asset is capital. This might apply, for example, to manufacturing firms. Here, since capital is most specialized, it is efficient to give capital "owner-ship" interests because specialized capital is most subject to expropria-tion through opportunistic behavior. Therefore, capital is the residual claimant and has the ultimate power to discipline (fire) other factors. In the firms discussed so far, capital has this role because it can most easily be exploited, and therefore is most in need of protection, or is willing to pay the most for protection.

But this is not true for all firms. Consider, for one example, a law firm. (Similar analysis applies to accounting and management consult-ing firms, and also to economic consulting firms.) Here, the most specialized assets are human capital, not physical capital. The physical capital used in such firms (desks, computers, libraries) is unspecialized and easily transferred, and of relatively low value compared to the value of the firm. The human capital, on the other hand, is highly valued, and makes up the bulk of the firm's value.

In this case, owners or suppliers of physical capital will not be the residual claimants. Rather, human capital owners will serve this func-tion. In this type of firm, we do indeed observe that labor (owners of human capital) performs the functions performed by owners of physical capital in other firms. These firms are commonly organized as partner-ships, and management control is vested in the hands of a committee of partners. The partners are the residual claimants in these firms. However, this structure is still subject to problems of opportunism. We will discuss the nature of these problems in the context of a law firm.*

Law Firms

In order to understand the problems associated with law firms, we must ask why lawyers organize themselves in firms, rather than simply remaining sole practitioners. The answer is in terms of diversification. It pays for lawyers to specialize because this increases productivity. However, the future value of a particular specialty cannot be determined at the time the investment is being made, and may fluctuate as a result of unpredictable forces. (For example, increased understanding of certain types of vertical contracts, as discussed in Chapter 6, may have caused a reduction in the value of antitrust lawyers. It would have been difficult to predict this at a time when many lawyers were investing in human capital needed for this specialty, perhaps by working for the Department of Justice or the Federal Trade Commission.) There may also be risks associated with specializing in the work associated with one client or industry.

As a result, lawyers can reduce their risk by forming associations (partnerships) including lawyers with different specialities. By forming such partnerships, the risks associated with specialization can be reduced. Because the purpose of the partnership is to diversify and thus reduce risks, earnings in these partnerships should be shared, perhaps as a function of seniority. But rules for sharing create risks of their own. Those lucky partners who turn out to have invested in the "right" specialties will have an incentive to break their contracts with unlucky lawyers who have invested wrongly. This is because the value of the lucky partners will turn out to be greater than their prorated share of earnings, since they are by definition the ones whose specialties paid off.

Sharing contracts can be broken either by the affected partners leaving the firm or by their demanding a larger share of income associated with the successful practice, a threat which is made meaningful by the possibility of leaving. Contractual solutions are not feasible because courts will not (and probably cannot) enforce contracts for specific performance. (Consider the difficulty in enforcing a contract

---

* From my own experience and observation, I can attest that similar issues arise in economics consulting firms, but there are less of these than there are law firms, and readers are less likely to have experience with an economics firm.

that states, "You will do the best job you can in litigating all of your cases.") If sharing is not feasible, then incentives for specialized investment in narrow skills will be reduced, and this is inefficient.

The solution is in terms of "firm-specific capital." To the extent that a law firm can develop capital which is associated with the firm, rather than with particular lawyers, incentives for leaving (and hence possibilities for grabbing) are reduced. Two major types of such capital are clients who "belong" to the firm, rather than to particular lawyers, and the reputation of the firm itself for performing quality work. Indeed, this reputation may be the major asset of the firm, since it is what assures clients of the value of the firm's human capital. Moreover, development of these firm-specific values is itself facilitated by a seniority-based pay system. However, it is not possible for all firms to accomplish this, which may indicate why lawyers still often leave senior positions at established firms. Moreover, the seniority-based pay system associated with this sharing itself creates incentive problems, particularly those associated with shirking.

Law firm organization must balance these various costs and benefits. The particular balance will depend on the type of practice. Firms with established long-term clients are more able to rely on sharing contracts, while firms with individuals or small businesses as clients may do better with pay schemes more closely reflecting direct productivity. It is interesting and consistent with the theory advanced here that many firms specializing in plaintiff's tort cases are basically organized as single practitioners. In these firms, there is little repeat business (so that clients do not belong to the firm in any sense) and reputations are those of important individuals so that pay reflects the value of these reputations.

ESOPS

One sometimes reads of proposals for employee ownership of firms. Employee Stock Ownership Plans (ESOPs) are advocated by some. In these plans, employees of firms with specialized physical capital, such as retailing firms or manufacturing firms, are given ownership rights. Advocates of these plans claim that this ownership will give employees incentives to maximize firm value.

This ownership structure has generally not arisen in competitive markets, unless it has been encouraged and subsidized (as through tax breaks) by government. (Recently there have been some efforts to create and use ESOPs to make hostile takeovers less likely to succeed.) This is because it is in general not an efficient structure. Few employees of a firm can meaningfully or significantly influence profits, so that giving them an ownership interest will have only trivial effects on motivation. This means that there are few benefits created. (Those employees who are powerful enough to have significant influence on profits are commonly rewarded with stock options or other rewards tied to performance.)

While there are few benefits, there are costs to giving employees ownership rights in the firm. These costs are borne by employees, most of whom would rather invest in firms other than the firm they work for. For most employees, a significant part of their wealth is the human capital invested in the firm. Because there are benefits of specialization, this is a significant nondiversifiable risk. (A full-time worker for one firm is worth enough more than a half-time worker for two firms to compensate for the risk.) Even where this is not true, there are costs from seeking new jobs. If the firm should shut down, employees will lose this capital, and will be forced to spend resources finding new employment, which may not be as desirable.

If employees' financial wealth is also invested in the firm (as is true if the employees own the firm) then in the event of the firm suffering hard times, the employees will lose their financial capital in addition to their human capital. General principles of risk diversification indicate that this arrangement is not optimal. Rather, it is generally more efficient for workers to invest their financial capital in areas unrelated to the investment of their human capital, which cannot be diversified.

It does not pay to encourage such inefficient (risk concentrating) forms of investment. If employees do invest in their own firms and therefore see their financial investments become riskier, they will demand additional compensation. In other words, workers will demand additional pay if, for example, their pension fund invests heavily in the employing firm. Managers should not encourage such investment except for those key employees who do make a perceptible difference in the performance of the firm. These are employees whose efforts are so firm-specific, and so difficult to monitor, that close alignment of ownership and management is the only solution to the principal-agent problem.

Single Proprietorships

Finally, we should note that many firms remain single proprietorships, owned and operated by a single individual or a family. Such firms are common in certain industries, such as restaurants. We would expect this structure in situations where shirking is easy, and difficult to detect, as is true of a business involving much use of cash. In such cases, single proprietorships are common. As discussed in Chapter 7, an alternative for such industries is franchising, where the individual enterprise is operated by an owner but there are gains from common reputations.

THE MARKET FOR MANAGEMENT

One additional constraint on managerial shirking is the management market itself. Managers develop reputations which can be more or less valuable in the marketplace. Managers who do not engage in shirking and who develop a reputation for maximizing the wealth of shareholders will have more profitable opportunities for future employment than managers who do shirk.

It is possible to use this market to enhance profitability and reduce shirking. For example, in setting up a new project, the firm may prominently indicate the particular manager who is going to run the project. This will serve two functions. First, by indicating that this manager has a past record as an efficient manager, the publicity will indicate that he is likely to do well again. Second, by advertising the name of the manager, the firm will be putting his reputation at risk. Investors will know that if there is opportunism and shirking in a project, the manager responsible will lose substantial reputational capital. Firms already indicate the names and functions of top management in the annual report, perhaps to serve this exact function. However, it might be useful to identify particular lower level managers responsible for particular projects in order to use reputation as an additional bond.

The firm can use the management market for an additional benefit. Managers within a firm may develop close relationships with each other, and may use these relationships for mutual shirking. By hiring outside managers, a firm can destroy these internal relationships, and perhaps increase profits. There are costs of hiring outside managers, in terms of teaching them the workings of the firm, but it may sometimes pay anyway as a way of reducing shirking.

SUMMARY

In a firm which is operated by the owner, there are no problems of shirking and no agency costs. However, as firms become larger and as there is debt or equity owned by persons other than the owner-manager, such problems arise.

For debt, the problem is this: If the firm goes bankrupt, debtors lose and the owner, the residual claimant, loses. If the firm invests in a risky activity and it is successful, the residual claimant gains but the debtors do not. Therefore, there is an asymmetry created, and firms financed by debt are likely to overinvest in risky activities. This problem is mitigated if the firm is relatively constrained in its activities, so that monitoring by auditors for bondholders is feasible. Active investors can also sometimes perform such monitoring.

Equity dilutes the interest of the managing owner in profits, and therefore creates its own agency problems. These can be in terms of on-the-job consumption, or in terms of inefficient investment patterns. In order to protect themselves, providers of equity obtain residual claimant status and control the firm. This control includes monitoring and the ability to fire top management through the board of directors. Another powerful control is the possibility of a takeover, discussed in the next chapter. Even so, there are residual possibilities for shirking.

The firm will in general be financed both by equity and debt, and by hybrids. A firm should use each source of finance until the marginal costs of each are equal. Overall, the size of the firm should be determined where the incremental cost of capital (for debt or equity) is just equal to the incremental returns from investment. Any additional earnings of the firm (free cash flow) should be returned to the stockholders. An intermediate form of finance is a closely held corporation, which has some of the advantages and some of the disadvantages of each form or organization. It is especially useful for raising more cash than may be possible with debt but not so much that public organization and trading of stocks is necessary.

When the most specialized asset of a firm is something other than physical capital, other factors may own the firm (serve as the residual claimant). Professional firms such as law firms are owned by the partners who also control the firm. The principles advanced in this book can explain features of law firm structure, such as reliance on pay based on seniority. Attempts to create incentives for other firms to mimic this structure, as by encouraging ESOPs, are misguided because risk becomes unnecessarily and inefficiently concentrated in the hands of workers when both human and financial capital are invested in the same firm. Firms in industries where shirking is easy and difficult to detect, such as restaurants, are commonly owned and operated by one individual because this minimizes the costs of shirking.

Finally, the market for management serves as an additional bond to control opportunism on the part of managers. Moreover, the firm can use this market to hire outside managers and destroy internal relationships between managers which may facilitate shirking.

REFERENCES

Alchian, Armen A., and Demsetz, Harold. "Production, Information Costs, and Economic Organization." *American Economic Review* 62 (1972):777. Reprinted in *The Economic Nature of the Firm,* edited by Louis Putterman.

Alchian, Armen A., and Woodward, Susan. "The Firm Is Dead; Long Live the Firm: A Review of Oliver E. Williamson's *The Economic Institutions of Capitalism.*" *The Journal of Economic Literature.* 26 (1988):65.

Coffee, John C., Jr., "Shareholders Versus Managers: The Strains in the Corporate Web." *Michigan Law Review* 85 (1986):1.

Demsetz, Harold, and Lehn, Kenneth. "The Structure of Corporate Ownership: Causes and Consequences." *Journal of Political Economy* 93 (1985):1155.

Easterbrook, Frank H., and Fischel, Daniel R. "Close Corporations and Agency Costs." *Stanford Law Review* 38 (1986):271.

Faith, Roger L.; Higgins, Richard S.; and Tollison, Robert D. "Managerial Rents and Outside Recruitment in the Coasian Firm." *American Economic Review* 74 (1984):660.

Fama, Eugene F. "Agency Problems and the Theory of the Firm." *Journal of Political Economy* 88 (1980):p. 288. Reprinted in *The Economic Nature of the Firm,* edited by Louis Putterman.

Gilson, Ronald J., and Mnookin, Robert H. "Sharing Among the Human Capitalists: An Economic Inquiry into the Corporate Law Firm and How Partners Split Profits." *Stanford Law Review* 37 (1985):313.

Jensen, Michael C., and Meckling, William H. "Theory of the Firm: Managerial Behavior, Agency Costs and Ownership Structure." *Journal of Financial Economics* 3 (1976):306. Reprinted in *The Economic Nature of the Firm,* edited by Louis Putterman.

Klein, Benjamin. "Contracting Costs and Residual Claims: The Separation of Ownership and Control." *Journal of Law and Economics* 26 (1983):367.

Klein, William A. "The Modern Business Organization: Bargaining Under Constraints." *The Yale Law Journal* 91 (1982):1521.

Mork, Randall; Shleifer, Andrei; and Vishnay, Robert W. "Altenative Mechanisms for Corporate Control." *American Economic Review* 79 (1989):842.

Pashigian, B. Peter. "Comment." *Stanford Law Review* 37 (1985):393.

Williamson, Oliver E. "Corporate Finance and Corporate Governance." *Journal of Finance* 43 (1988):567.

– 5 –

Takeovers and
Restructurings

A takeover is a change in the ownership of a firm. Takeovers are financial transactions, and the principles of finance, discussed in the last chapter, are directly relevant for understanding takeovers. In fact, this chapter may be viewed as a continuation of the last; an analysis of takeovers is a branch of finance.

For a manager, there are two central issues involving takeovers. The most important is, "How should I run my firm to avoid being taken over?" A second issue is, "Under what circumstances should I attempt to acquire another firm?" (although this is less likely to be an important issue for many managers). There are also subsidiary issues dealing with reactions to potential and actual acquisitions.

There are several types of takeovers. In a leveraged buy out or other "going private" transaction, a group of investors, often including incumbent management, buys the equity of stockholders and replaces it with debt, so that the company is no longer a publicly traded corporation. In a merger, the terms of the takeover are negotiated by the managements of the firms involved, and the agreement is given to stockholders for ratification. A tender offer is an offer directly from one firm to stockholders of the target firm. Tender offers are said to be "friendly" if they are approved by the target's management, and "hostile" otherwise. Proxy contests are attempts by a dissident management team to convince stockholders to vote for them.

Firms may merge for several reasons. There may be synergies between the products made by the two firms. An aging owner of a firm may want to sell out to retire or create an estate for his family. A firm may develop a product line with the expectation of selling out to others. And there are many more. However, since this book deals with opportunism, the focus is on one particular set of motives. But the reader should keep in mind that these motives are not the only, or even the major, reasons for mergers.

In what follows, there is often reference to the effects on stock-holders of particular provisions. These effects are measured by what is called an *event study*. This is a technique used by economists and specialists in finance to examine the effect of a particular event on the stock. The analyst uses statistical techniques to isolate the particular event under consideration, and then looks at the effect on stock prices and values of the event. Generally, effects will be seen in the stock market within a few days of the occurrence of the event. This technique is able to separate out general market movements from movements of the particular stock under consideration. This is the most objective method now available to determine the effects of policies on stock-holders. In the appendix, some additional possibilities are discussed for the use of event studies.

Before beginning the substantive discussion of changes in owner-ship of firms, an important caveat is in order.

A CAVEAT

As we shall see, the best current theory of takeovers (and that which is the foundation for the analysis in this chapter) is based on the notion that takeovers occur when management is shirking and not behaving so as to maximize stockholder wealth. The way to avoid being taken over is then not to shirk, but rather to maximize shareholder wealth. This also has the advantage of being economically efficient and therefore socially desirable.

There are other strategies available to managers to avoid takeovers, however. Incumbent management can litigate and use the legal system to try to block potential takeovers. In litigating, targets attempting to block takeovers have alleged securities fraud, violation of federal or state tender offer requirements, and antitrust laws. This litigation sometimes benefits stockholders by giving other bidders time to make better offers for targets, but in other cases it is associated with losses to shareholders of targets. It is also possible and not uncommon for managers to lobby state legislatures for legislation which protects their position and makes takeovers more difficult. Passage of such legislation is associated with losses in value to shareholders of firms incorporated in the state passing the legislation. Other strategies include "poison pills" and "greenmail," discussed in further detail below.

These strategies are sometimes nonmaximizing, in that they result in an inefficient transfer from owners to managers, with associated *deadweight losses*. (That is, the gains to managers are less than the loss to shareholders.) In what follows, I will deal only with efficient behavior. While some managers may want guidance in the use of inefficient methods of protecting their positions, they will not find such guidance here. Rather, I will concentrate on efficient adaptations. However, remember that efficient behavior maximizes the total gains from a transaction. It is generally possible to find ways of making *both* parties to an efficient transaction better off than under an inefficient transaction.* Managers and stockholders should be able to gain from structuring contracts in the sorts of ways discussed in this book. There will still be cases in which issues arise as to the division of the gains between managers and stockholders, and I discuss some of these situations, but without resolving the questions. However, in general I follow the policy in this book of assuming the existence of opportunism, but not encouraging it, particularly in those cases where it leads to inefficiency.

GOING PRIVATE: CONVERSION OF EQUITY TO DEBT

In recent years, a common form of business reorganization has been an increase in various forms of "going private," a situation in which a public corporation becomes privately held and in which equity (stock) finance is replaced by debt. The most common form of this transition is the "leveraged buyout," or LBO. In an LBO, a group of investors, generally including incumbent top management, buys the firm from its stockholders. The buyout is generally financed by debt (so it is "leveraged"). It is common for the debt to be financed by junk bonds. Commonly, after the transaction, the firm will be restructured. Often after a successful reorganization and recapitalization the LBO will again be sold as a public corporation offering stock, though this is not always the case. When a firm is operated as an LBO, the financial firm organizing the transaction will remain as an active investor—one who actively participates in monitoring the firm.

A going-private transaction may not affect an entire firm. Another possibility is for a firm which does not go private in its entirety to spin off

---

* Strictly speaking, this is not always true. However, in cases where parties are already transacting with each other, as in contractual situations, there should be mechanisms available for accomplishing this goal.

some divisions as LBOs to their own management. After an entire firm undergoes an LBO, it will sometimes be split up into separate LBOs, sold to their respective managements.

All of these features can be explained in terms of issues already discussed. Moreover, by understanding the relevant issues, a manager can determine when such a move is likely to be in his and his firm's interests. What is happening in these cases is the replacement of equity with debt. This can be explained in terms of the distinction made earlier between the properties of debt and equity. The goal is the reduction of managerial shirking, as explained below. Debt, by requiring a fixed payment, limits the incentive for shirking because managers retain residual-claimant status and because payments for debt service do not allow shirking. Since debt payments are contractual, the existence of debt forces managers to pay out the profits of the firm, rather than retaining them. (This of course applies to debt used to repay borrowing which is not retained as cash by the firm.)

The disadvantage of debt is the incentive for management to undertake investments which are too risky, since owner-managers gain from profitable investments but do not lose as much in the event of bankruptcy. There are several factors limiting this possibility in an LBO. First, since managers in an LBO have substantial ownership interests, the disadvantage of debt in terms of its incentive for overly risky speculation is limited because managers would also lose from bankruptcy. Second, other creditors, including the financial firm responsible for organizing the LBO, have sufficiently large interests so that they can engage in substantial monitoring of the LBO to make sure that overly risky activities are avoided. Moreover, financial firms specializing in organizing LBOs have valuable reputations. These reputations enable them to raise capital for additional LBOs. Therefore, they would spend more on monitoring any given LBO than might be warranted from the narrow perspective of their investment in the particular endeavor in order to preserve this valuable reputation.

Finally, the purpose of the LBO is often restructuring in order to eliminate waste. During the period of restructuring, the LBO will have no reason to undertake speculative or risky new investments; managerial efforts will be devoted to the restructuring. During this period, when the firm is operated as an LBO and debtors are vulnerable, the firm will be undertaking few if any of the sorts of investments in major new activities which would carry risks of bankruptcy. When the restructuring is over and the firm begins normal operations, it will often be restored as a corporation, with the associated policing and reduction in incentives for overly risky investment.

Why does such a restructuring pay? The possibility of earning positive returns from restructuring is usually the result of a failure of the board of directors to police management efficiently. That is, LBOs are common in situations where management has shirked or behaved opportunistically. One common form of such agency problems is the overexpansion of the firm into relatively unprofitable areas, which are often unrelated to the original line of business. There are benefits to management from such overexpansion, since managers always prefer to run a larger enterprise, but there are costs to stockholders. An LBO can be profitable because it eliminates incentives for such inefficient expansion. This can also explain why it is common for LBOs to sell off divisions of the firm. The divisions which are sold are those which had been inefficiently acquired by management. Similarly, when public firms spin off divisions as LBOs, they are removing divisions which can be more efficiently managed as free-standing enterprises and which have probably been inefficiently acquired by growth seeking management.

The issue is sometimes characterized as excess "free cash flow." Free cash flow is cash flow earned by a firm over and above any cash which can profitably be invested at the relevant cost of capital. The interests of stockholders are in having such cash returned to them since by definition the firm cannot profitably invest it. However, there is an agency problem in that management will often want to run a larger firm than is optimal, and the investment of free cash flow in relatively unprofitable activities will serve these management goals.

This problem is particularly acute in industries which generate substantial amounts of cash but in which there is little growth and little opportunity for profitable investment, and these are the industries (often major manufacturing industries) in which LBOs have been most common. Some examples of industries meeting these characteristics are tire, steel, chemical, brewing, broadcasting, paper, as well as many other manufacturing industries. In these cases, the industries are relatively mature, so that there is little benefit from additional growth (and perhaps some benefit from downsizing), and the industry generates substantial cash flow. These are all cases where some form of going private can be efficient because it can reduce or eliminate the inefficient use of free cash flow.

There are two possible explanations for the current increase in LBOs; they may be related. One is that the creation of the junk bond market has provided a source of debt capital which can be used for financing LBOs. A second possibility is that fear of takeovers (discussed in detail below, but perhaps due to junk bonds as well) has caused management to seek ways of avoiding hostile takeovers, and a restructuring into an LBO, since it achieves the goals of a takeover, will prevent one from occurring.

There is another circumstance, in addition to misappropriation of free cash flow, in which going private may be worthwhile. We indicated above that nonspecialized capital can most easily be financed through debt because creditors can easily seize such capital and therefore it is good collateral. A company might grow through the use of equity. However, if it uses mainly nonspecialized capital, once it has stopped growing, it may be efficient to restructure it and finance it through debt. An LBO is a mechanism for achieving this new equilibrium. It is also possible that some investment projects of the firm could most profitably be undertaken by an entity other than the firm, so that it will be efficient simply to reorganize the firm. In this case, an LBO might be the best vehicle for the reorganization. The returns to management from the LBO is then the reward for undertaking the restructuring, which may be risky.

The advantage to a manager of an LBO over a hostile takeover is that the LBO will preserve the jobs of incumbent managers. Of course, to the extent that there is less shirking, these jobs may be less desirable. However, since incumbent management can make substantial profits from a successful LBO, management will still generally gain. The reason why LBOs can be so profitable is precisely because they eliminate the incentive for shirking, and shirking is by definition inefficient.

As a manager, when should you propose or consider an LBO? Essentially, when you perceive that there are profitable possibilities for restructuring the firm and squeezing out excess costs or selling superfluous divisions. Under these circumstances, an LBO may be quite profitable. These profits will in part flow to shareholders, since they will be paid a premium to sell their shares to the LBO, and the announcement of a management buyout raises stock prices by about 20 percent on average. Part of the profits will flow to investors who invest in the LBO, including the financial firms organizing the deal. However, those managers in sufficiently senior positions to participate in the transaction will often reap substantial rewards as well. There is room for gains to many parties because the LBO structure is more efficient than the public corporation, and the essence of efficiency is the creation of returns which can be divided among participants.

Another option for incumbent managers is a leveraged recapitalization, or "recap." In this scenario, managers pay a large dividend to stockholders. This dividend is essentially the value of the company, including both the market value of the stock and any additional value hidden in the misappropriation of free clash flow. The payment is financed through debt. It is similar to an LBO, but incumbent management does not need to come up with capital for the deal. An additional benefit, of course, is that incumbent management does not lose their jobs. A firm undergoing a recap is generally kept public, and the recap is followed by a new stock issue.

Some say that LBOs are wrong because they are ways of paying managers to maximize the value of the company and managers should do this anyway. However, an important premise of this book and the underlying analysis is that there are in general incentives for shirking and for opportunistic behavior. Such behavior is neither particularly moral nor immoral. The proper reaction is not moralistic, but rather the structuring of incentives to eliminate the costs of such shirking. LBOs and other devices discussed in this chapter are aimed at reducing this inefficiency.

HOW TO AVOID BEING TAKEN OVER

There is substantial evidence that takeovers increase the returns to stockholders of the acquired company. This is a strong indication that firms are being run inefficiently, and the gains from acquisitions accrue because the acquiring company plans to run the firm more efficiently. Much of the gain is from the elimination of shirking and particularly the misuse of free cash flow.

The first point to note is that, since takeovers occur to avoid problems of shirking, the simplest way to avoid a takeover is not to shirk. The most significant form of shirking is probably the misuse of free cash flow. This is most significant in the sense that it is most costly for the firm and the economy and also in the sense that it is the behavior which is most likely to make a firm the object of a successful hostile takeover. Since free cash flow is money which cannot profitably be invested in the firm, the only efficient policy is to return this money to the stockholders as dividend payments or stock repurchases so that the stockholders can themselves invest the money. Any other use, such as investment in areas which do not pay the true cost of capital to the firm, is inefficient. Therefore, the first rule to avoid being taken over is, "Return free cash flow to the shareholders." Firms whose managers obey this rule will be unlikely to be taken over.

However, for a manager, this rule is not simple to obey. First, only the top manager can control shirking and the use of cash flow for the firm in its entirety. Second, even he will have some difficulty since as firms become large there are agency problems created between various managers; control within a firm is not perfect. As a result, the CEO will not always fully know the rate of return to be expected from investments proposed by subordinates, and it will not be easy (inexpensive) to find out; this difficulty is the essence of an agency problem. Third, human beings have a tendency to perceive things which benefit themselves as being good, so that some behavior which is actually inefficient would not be so perceived by the decision maker if he will benefit from the behavior. Managers may propose particular investments and truly believe that they are worthwhile, even when an objective observer with all the facts would think that they were not. (For another example, many managers claim that the recent increase in takeovers is harmful, and many of them undoubtedly believe that this is so.) All these things mean that it will be difficult for the management of a firm to correctly determine when cash flow is indeed free.

The alternative to a rule such as that proposed above is for incumbent management to create a set of incentives or a structure of the firm which will lead managers, acting in their own interest, to avoid shirking. When contracts cause managers to avoid shirking, their lives are somewhat less pleasant because by definition shirking creates utility for the shirker. For example, it is better to be the CEO of a $500 million firm than of a $400 million firm, even if the profits of the latter are proportionally greater.

However, there are compensations. First, a firm with no shirking is more profitable, and some of the gains can go to management. Thus, the contract which leads to avoidance of shirking can also entail higher compensation. Amenities may be lower and managers may work harder, but they will be paid more. Second, firms in which management shirks may be taken over, and the result of such a takeover is often the replacement of large numbers of managers. Therefore, the choice may be between being a nonshirking manager and not being a manager at all. In this case, the efficient nonshirking conduct is clearly superior.

There are various alternatives for structuring managerial contracts to avoid shirking. One possibility, discussed above, is for the firm to go private through some means such as an LBO. Once the firm becomes private and is financed through debt, then the forced interest payments associated with the large outstanding debt will force the managers to return free cash flow to bondholders or creditors. Even if the firm decides not to go private, it is possible to borrow some of the techniques used by successful firms which have gone private in structuring contracts for managers which reduce incentives for shirking.

One feature of an efficient managerial contract is relating pay directly to performance, not to the size of the firm. If pay is related to size, then managers have an incentive to make the firm too large, as by inefficiently investing free cash flow. If pay is related to actual cash flow and other measures of performance, then proper incentives are created for efficient operation.

A second principle is to rely heavily on debt finance. Debt which is not retained as cash forces the firm to pay out earnings, rather than retaining them. Moreover, if the firm wants to invest in some opportunity which it believes will be profitable, use of debt will force the firm to go to the capital market for finance. If the project cannot be funded in this way, it is probably not worthwhile. If it can receive funding, then it may be worthwhile. If the funding is through debt, then there will be an immediate check on the profitability of the project. If the firm cannot meet its contractually required payments, the project was likely a mistake, and the best strategy is to close it down quickly. Debt will also meet this goal since repayments must be made as scheduled. (This does not mean that payments must begin immediately; it is possible to schedule debt repayments to begin only after some time has passed. However, the project must show positive earnings at the time when it planned to do so.)

A corollary is that firms should not use the earnings of one division to finance projects in another. Each part of the firm should pay its own way. This will minimize possibilities for diverting free cash flow from profitable to unprofitable divisions. Another point is that firms should undertake investments primarily in areas closely related to their primary business. If investors in the steel industry want to invest some of their profits in the retailing business, they can do so directly if the profits are returned to them. There is no benefit from having the officers of a steel company undertake this investment for the stockholders, and there are likely some costs. While there may be some circumstances where investment in unrelated activities is justified, it is much more likely that such investment is a misuse of free cash flow, and the market is likely to detect this and punish the managers accordingly.

Note also that nothing has been said about long-term versus short-term investment. Many believe that firms are penalized for making long-term investments, and that there is too much pressure for short-term results in contemporary American business. Incumbent managers lose from hostile takeovers, and as a result they often claim that such takeovers are inefficient. One such claim is that firms are forced to invest in short-term projects to avoid being taken over, and that the market over-rewards short-term earnings, at the expense of long-term returns. However, there is no evidence that this is so. For example, there is evidence that firms engaging in efficient R & D are less likely to be taken over than other firms, and that the market price of stock rises when efficient investment programs are announced.

There is some evidence that takeovers are more likely in industries which are doing poorly. This may be the result of unwillingness by top managers and boards of directors to eliminate excess employees. While it may seem heartless to fire managers who are competent and able because the industry is declining, the result of not eliminating excess employees may be a takeover, in which the managers will be fired anyway. Moreover, economics indicates that reduction of employment in declining industries is efficient and will maximize the value of society's wealth, even though some particular persons will lose.

SHOULD YOU TAKE OVER A FIRM?

The second question facing a manager is the issue of taking over some other firm. In general, firms which have engaged in takeovers have not done particularly well for their shareholders. This does not mean that one should never engage in a takeover. However, it does indicate caution.

The first and most important point to keep in mind is that the existence of profitable activities is not itself enough to justify investing the capital of stockholders in these activities. There must be some explicit, concrete reason why these investments are more profitable for your firm than for anyone else. In general there will be competition for the assets of the acquired firm. Others in addition to you will be bidding on these assets. Therefore, unless the target is worth more to you than to others, there is no reason to expect a better-than-average return on the investment required in the takeover. If there is no reason, then the stockholders can invest their wealth themselves after you return it to them. They do not need you as an intermediary.

Second, a takeover can itself be a way of misusing free cash flow. That is, some takeovers may be inefficient and may misuse the capital of the firm. If you as a manager are aware that this is the purpose of a takeover, you should not do it, but rather you should return the money to your stockholders. Of course, it may not always be possible to determine if a takeover is efficient or not. Most importantly, it is more likely that a takeover is efficient if the target is a firm in approximately the same industry as the acquirer. Over the last twenty years, we have learned that excess diversification is not efficient and does not pay. Thus, as a manager, you should be extremely skeptical if a subordinate tells you that an acquisition in an unrelated industry will truly benefit stockholders. You should be just as skeptical if you come to this conclusion yourself. Moreover, there is a risk in attempting inefficient takeovers because there is evidence that firms which engage in such actions are themselves likely to be candidates for being taken over.

Third, you should have a very good idea as to the gains from the acquisition. It is best if you can pinpoint explicit cost savings or other benefits which will result. The more specifically the savings and benefits can be identified, the more likely that it is that there are real savings, and the less likely that you have been fooled, or have fooled yourself. Even if you anticipate transacting with the acquired firm (if, for example, it produces some input which you are currently buying on the open market), you should be sure that there are benefits from common ownership. One way to approach this problem is to try to determine in advance exactly what structure you will use for intrafirm transactions after the acquisition has occurred. If, for example, you anticipate that arms-length transactions will be the most efficient, then this is a sign that there are few if any benefits from the acquisition, as discussed in Chapter 3.

RELATED ISSUES

In reading the financial press, one is struck with the number of picturesque terms—*golden parachutes, greenmail, shark repellents,* and *poison pills*—that are apparently normal forms of corporate commerce related to facilitating or hindering efforts at transfer of ownership of a firm. In this section, each of these terms is briefly discussed in relation to the issues already identified. The reader should note that there is rapid evolution in these institutions, and the evidence about their effects is often preliminary. Firms are continually adopting variants of these provisions, and analysts are attempting to measure the effects of these variants using event studies. What is known, as of now, about various provisions will be summarized, but the reader should note that by the time he reads this additional provisions will probably have been created, and additional studies of their effects will probably exist in the literature. Thus, this section is brief and by nature of an introduction, not a definitive summary.

The issues under discussion deal with efforts by incumbent management to make takeovers more difficult. However, in general, it is important to note that the efficient behavior of incumbent managers is to maximize the value of the stock of the firm. Some efforts to reduce takeovers (such as lobbying for passage of state laws making takeovers more difficult) clearly harm stockholders, and, while they may benefit incumbent management, are at least irresponsible. Much litigation regarding takeovers also reduces stockholder wealth. Other provisions, including those discussed below, may benefit shareholders indirectly by allowing additional bids from other outsiders (sometimes called "white knights"). But there is little justification for policies aimed at benefiting management at the expense of shareholders. More importantly, there are net gains from restructuring contracts so as to eliminate the costs of the inefficiencies created when managers are benefitted at stockholders' expense.

An important but unresolved issue is the relation between seeking additional bids and the ultimate benefit to stockholders. Provisions which make takeovers more difficult have two effects. Once a takeover attempt has been announced, such provisions increase the value of payments received by the shareholders because they enable incumbent management to "shop" the firm (that is, seek additional bidders) and increase the value expected to be received by shareholders. Thus, once an announcement of a takeover has been made, these provisions are beneficial.

However, these same provisions reduce the incentive for potential bidders to make a bid in the first place, and thus reduce the value to shareholders. Consider a potential buyer, Company B, contemplating an offer for Company S. The first decision B must make is whether to invest the resources in determining if S is a good buy. If it is known that Company S has a provision on the books which will enable its management to shop the company and seek competing bids from other potential buyers once an offer has been made, then it is less valuable for B to make the investment in deciding to bid on S. This is because there is some chance that someone else will buy S as a result of the bidding process, and even if B does win the auction, it will pay a higher price than without the provision, thus lowering its returns.

A similar issue is implicitly involved with respect to LBOs. If managers know that their offer of a price associated with an LBO will be shopped, they are less likely to make an offer. If the offer cannot be shopped, there are strong incentives for making too low an offer and obtaining more of the gains of the transaction for themselves at the expense of the shareholders. There are methods of monitoring this offer (e.g., the board can determine if it is too low), but none are as effective as the open market.

Thus, the theory is ambiguous. Provisions which make takeovers more difficult might increase the value of the company by enabling managers to obtain higher values once bidding has begun, or they might reduce the value of the company by reducing the chance of an offer being made in the first place. In our discussion of particular institutions, we see that the ambiguity applies to the measurement of effects of such provisions on shareholder wealth. Part of the ambiguity may be due to the fact that different types of corporations and different shareholders may differ with respect to the value of such provisions. Therefore, in some contexts, adopting the provisions may benefit shareholders, while in others they may not. In what follows, what is known about the effects of these provisions will be indicated, but a great deal of guidance cannot be given even to those managers interested in maximizing shareholder wealth.

Golden Parachutes

This refers to a contract giving corporate officers large severance payments in the event of a takeover. As a manager, you should find such payments desirable, and it is fortunate that they can be efficient as well. There are two functions served by such contracts.

First, it was indicated above (Chapter 3) that compensation of managers often includes noncontractual expected future payments. These can be efficient as methods of rewarding managers who turn out to be more productive and efficient than was anticipated. Such payments can be viewed as compensation for this added efficiency. They are noncontractual because when a manager is hired, it is impossible to know her productivity. Nonetheless, productive managers may have reasonable expectations regarding such rewards. The board of directors has an incentive to satisfy these expectations because these payments make recruitment and retention of competent managers easier.

In the event of a takeover, however, the new board has little or no incentive to honor these implicit agreements, since they were agreements with the board of the acquired company. However, if managers come to learn that these implicit contracts will not be kept, then incentives for efficient performance will be reduced. Thus, one function of golden parachutes is to reward efficient performance, and to provide incentives for such performance. A manager working for a firm with such a contract will be motivated to perform efficiently. Additionally, Chapter 3 showed that some contracts involve posting of a "bond" by managers which is returned if the manager does not shirk. A golden parachute can be a way of returning this bond to appropriate managers.

The second function is the creation of incentives for managers to agree to efficient takeovers. Incumbent managers of target firms can often lose as a result of a hostile takeover. This is particularly likely if the goal of the takeover is the liquidation of the firm, as discussed in the last chapter, but it can occur in other circumstances as well. There are also ways in which such managers can block takeovers, or at least make them less likely. During negotiations about takeovers, managers are being asked to negotiate something for the stockholders which is probably not in the best interests of the managers themselves. The creation of golden parachutes creates incentives for managers to continue maximizing stockholder wealth, and makes it in the interest of incumbent management of target firms to encourage or allow efficient transfers of ownership. (The ethics of rewarding managers for nonshirking behavior was discussed earlier.)

Thus, for two reasons, these provisions may be efficient. However, it is important that they be limited to those managers who can effect the likelihood of a successful takeover, and who have accrued noncontractual expectations from the firm. Nonetheless, when management has the option of either building a golden parachute or adopting an inefficient antitakeover provision in order to protect their jobs, the golden parachute is clearly preferable because it enables management and shareholders to share in efficiency gains, rather than blocking the realization of these gains.

Greenmail

Greenmail is the buying back of stock from certain specified purchasers. The technical name is "targeted block stock repurchases." The target firm will pay a premium for the shares of a potential buyer of the firm who holds a large block of stock. The purpose may be to enable the managers to receive a higher price from other buyers, although the fear is that it is used by shirking managers to protect their jobs.

The analysis of the effects of greenmail is complex. The best evidence now indicates that from the beginning of a takeover attempt until the paying of the greenmail, stockholders of targets benefit. There is some evidence that the ability of a firm to pay greenmail makes acquisition of its stock by outsiders interested in making profits by improving the efficiency of the firm more likely, and thus benefits stockholders. Moreover, if the paying of greenmail to one potential acquirer ultimately leads to another firm acquiring the stock of the target at a price above that offered by the greenmail recipient, stockholders benefit. Greenmail may be viewed as compensation to those who have accumulated the information that the stock of the firm is undervalued. However, if the result of greenmail is to eliminate the possibility of a takeover and if incumbent management does not respond by more efficient behavior, the result is a loss to stockholders. This may be unlikely, however, because if managers have paid greenmail once for this purpose, this information is public and it is possible for others to engage in similar transactions.

Shark Repellents

This term is used for various proposals which require "supermajorities" (ranging from 66 to 90 percent) of stockholders to approve hostile tender offers. They come in various forms, with various efficiency implications.

Pure supermajority amendments are inefficient, in that they reduce the value of the firm. They are commonly passed by firms with substantial insider ownership. However, recently this form of antitakeover provision has been less common, perhaps because it requires stockholder approval and one would not expect stockholders to approve of transactions which reduce their wealth.

A modified form of a supermajority amendment is a "fair price amendment." This eliminates the supermajority requirement when a tender offer is at a "fair" price, where fair is often defined as the highest price paid by the acquirer for any stock. These amendments seem to have little significant effect on stock prices.

Poison Pills

The strongest antitakeover provisions, these are shareholder rights agreements that are triggered by an event such as a tender offer. When triggered, these agreements provide shareholders with rights to purchase additional shares or to sell shares to the target. They serve to make takeovers very expensive, and substantially discourage hostile tenders offers. Anyone wanting to buy the firm will be forced to negotiate with management and acquire the firm on a friendly basis. Adopting these policies is associated with small but significant losses to shareholders of targets.

Changes in State Law

Sometimes managers under attack or fearing an attack will lobby state legislatures to attempt to change the law in the state to make takeovers more difficult. Managers can undertake such lobbying without shareholder approval. Since managers and workers who would benefit from inefficient changes in takeover regulations are residents of the relevant state and shareholders may live anywhere, state legislatures might approve inefficient regulations. Indeed, there is evidence that changes in state law affecting takeovers tend to reduce the value of stock. On the other hand, there is evidence that shifting the state of incorporation (which must be approved by shareholders) generally increases shareholder wealth.

States differ widely in their policies with respect to corporations, including takeover policies. Therefore, for any given set of policies which management might want, there is probably a state which offers something very close to this set of policies. If management wants to change the rules governing takeovers of stock in the company, an efficient policy is to shift the state of incorporation to a state offering the desired package, rather than lobbying the legislature to change the rules. If stockholders do not vote for the change, it is likely not in their interests.

SUMMARY

Takeovers of various forms are methods of changing the ownership of a firm. They are the ultimate form of discipline for managers. The effects of takeovers are measured through "event studies." This chapter discusses only efficient reactions to takeovers.

In recent years, many firms have used leveraged buyouts to convert equity finance to debt. Often these LBOs have been financed through high yield bonds, called junk bonds. This conversion can solve some of the agency problems associated with appropriation by the managers of a firm of free cash flow. Spinoffs of divisions associated with LBOs are generally signs that management invested in some activities for which the firm was not suited, and such restructurings are generally efficient.

To avoid having your firm taken over, the best strategy is not to appropriate free cash flow. However, this policy is difficult to establish by rule. A more effective policy is to structure incentives so there is little reward for misuse of free cash flow. One policy is to reward managers for performance, not for growth of the firm. Heavy use of debt finance is also a way of limiting misuse of free cash flow. The firm should avoid using the profits of one division to subsidize other divisions, and should expand in directions related to current activities. Contrary to some popular wisdom, there is no evidence that firms which invest for long-term profits are penalized, and some evidence that they are not, so that a manager wanting to avoid being acquired should not invest with an inefficiently short-time horizon.

Taking over another firm is a risky proposition, in that firms engaging in takeovers have not done particularly well for their stockholders. You should only acquire another firm if it is in a related business and if there are clear identifiable gains from such an acquisition.

In determining the optimal policy with respect to takeovers, there is a dilemma. Policies which make takeovers more difficult mean that when a takeover occurs, the price will be higher but takeovers will be less likely to occur. The balance of these factors is not clear. Several devices are used to make being acquired more difficult; these include golden parachutes (payment to incumbent managers in the event of a takeover), greenmail (stock repurchases from a potential acquirer), shark repellents (various forms of supermajority requirements for acquisition), and poison pills (provisions leading to stock dilution in the case of a takeover). Golden parachutes can be efficient, and poison pills are generally inefficient. The other options are more complex, and their efficiency varies with conditions.

In the appendix, I propose that a firm consider using "event studies" of the effects of announcing various policy proposals on the stock of the company to determine if the proposals are in the interests of stockholders.

REFERENCES

Baysinger, Barry D., and Butler, Henry N. "Antitakeover Amendments, Managerial Entrenchment, and the Contractual Theory of the Corporation. *Virginia Law Review* 71 (1985): 1257.

Jarrell, Gregg A.; Brickley, James A., and Netter, Jeffrey M. "The Market for Corporate Control: The Empirical Evidence Since 1980." *Journal of Economic Perspectives* 2 (1980): 49.

Jensen, Michael C. "Agency Costs of Free Cash Flow, Corporate Finance, and Takeovers." *American Economic Review* 76 (1986): 323.

Jensen, Michael C. "Eclipse of the Public Corporation." *Harvard Business Review.* (Sept./Oct. 1989): 61.

Jensen, Michael C. "Takeovers: Their Causes and Consequences." *Journal of Economic Perspectives* 2 (1988): 21.

Jensen, Michael, C. and Meckling, William H. "Theory of the Firm: Managerial Behavior, Agency Costs and Ownership Structure." *Journal of Financial Economics* 3 (1976): 306. Reprinted in *The Economic Nature of the Firm,* edited by Louis Putterman.

Kieschnick, Robert L., Jr. "Management Buyouts of Public Corporations: An Analysis of Prior Characteristics." In *Leveraged Management Buyouts,* edited by Yakov Amihud. Homewood, Ill.: Dow Jones-Irwin, 1989.

Knoeber, Charles R. "Golden Parachutes, Shark Repellents, and Hostile Tender Offers." *American Economic Review* 76 (1986): 155.

Lehn, Kenneth, and Mitchell, Mark. "Do Bad Bidders Become Good Targets." *Journal of Political Economy* 98 (1990): 372.

Macey, Jonathan R., and McChesney, Fred S. "A Theoretical Analysis of Corporate Greenmail." *Yale Law Journal* 95 (1985): 13.

Manne, Henry. "Mergers and the Market for Corporate Control." *Journal of Political Economy* (1965): 110.

Mork, Randall; Shleifer, Andrei; and Vishnay, Robert W. "Alternative Mechanisms for Corporate Control." *American Economic Review* 79 (1989): 842.

Schwert, G. William. "Using Financial Data to Measure the Effects of Regulation." *Journal of Law and Economics* 24 (1981): 121.

Segal, Harvey H. *Corporate Makeover: The Reshaping of the American Economy.* New York: Viking, 1989.

Williamson, Oliver E. "Transaction Cost Economics." In *Handbook of Industrial Organization,* edited by Richard Schmalensee and Robert Willig. New York: North Holland, 1989.

APPENDIX

In this appendix, I present a proposal for the use of event studies. So far as I know, the use I suggest has not been tried by firms, so that this proposal is somewhat more speculative than most of the material in the book.

The effects of the antitakeover policies referred to above have been measured through event studies. These have typically been done by academic economists and professors of finance; many of the results referred to here have been derived by economists at the Office of the Chief Economist of the Securities and Exchange Commission. To my knowledge, firms have not used such studies as decision-making tools. However, there is no reason not to do so. A firm could make an announcement of the following sort: "We are considering adding a provision to our charter which would require a 66 percent majority for approval of a tender offer unless the offer is at a fair price. Our decision will depend on the reaction of stockholders." The firm could then wait a few days and perform an event study. If the price of the stock increased relative to the market, the policy could be adopted; if it decreased, the policy would not be adopted. If there was no significant change, the management could do what it preferred.

Such studies could actually be used for many types of decision making. They would be useful for any major decision contemplated by a firm. For example, before a firm initiated an acquisition of another firm a similar study could be done. Event studies could also be used to evaluate major investment projects, or other changes in firm structure or behavior.

There would be two advantages to this form of decision making. First, the firm would undertake no action which lowered the stock value, so that it would always behave consistently with shareholders' interests. Second, the firm would have the benefit of the entire stock market in evaluating proposals, and the wisdom of the market is greater than the wisdom of any management team. The market would quickly learn to discount any announcement which was aimed at seeking information since such announcements would only indicate a possibility of some event occurring. However, since there would be a positive probability of the suggestion actually occurring, the direction of change in the stock price should be correct even if the magnitude were to be too small. The market would discount the probability of the event, but it would not discount it to zero.

PART III
Marketing

$-6-$

Distributing the Product:
Vertical Controls

A "manufacturer" (or "producer") makes some product which will be sold to individual consumers for use as a final product. The problems facing the manufacturer are many. For example, how should distribution from the manufacturer to the final consumer be handled? Should there be any restrictions placed on sale of the product after it leaves the hands of the manufacturer, and if so what sort of restrictions? This, in particular, is a complex problem. There are many possible solutions and many variables to consider in choosing which is best. Variables include both the form in which products are sold and restrictions placed on final sellers of products (called "retailers" or "dealers").*

Here are a few of the types of distribution arrangements that have been used by some manufacturers: integrating directly into retailing, establishing exclusive dealers who are allowed to sell only the products of the manufacturer, establishing franchises (discussed in the next chapter), and establishing departments within retail stores for selling the products of the manufacturer. Moreover, manufacturers have also established many restrictions on the behavior of retailers (when there is no direct vertical integration into retailing). Some restrictions are: maximum and minimum retail prices at which sales are allowed,†

---

*Many of the restrictions discussed in this chapter have been held illegal under the antitrust laws, although most economists who have studied the matter believe that the restrictions are in general efficient and in consumers' interests. Before adopting any of the policies discussed here, it is a good idea to discuss them with an antitrust attorney. One purpose of this chapter will be to indicate alternative methods of achieving the same goals. It should also be noted that antitrust law is in a state of flux and is becoming more favorable to efficient arrangements.

†Restrictions on pricing are in many circumstances illegal under the antitrust laws, and it is particularly important to discuss any such restrictions with an attorney.

restrictions on the territory in which dealers are allowed to sell, requirements of certain methods of retailing and on services (e.g., shelf space, location in the store, number of sales persons) required by retailers, limitations of the number of dealers in a given area, and requirements that dealers carry only the product of a given manufacturer.

There are several points to keep in mind in analyzing these restrictions. First, it is impossible to write complete contracts. That is, a manufacturer who wants a retailer to behave in a certain way cannot write a contract which will correctly specify all elements of the retailer's behavior. Second, vertical integration may be costly and in many cases will not pay. For one reason, there are substantial possibilities for shirking at the retail level and it may be prohibitively costly for a manufacturer to monitor the behavior of retailers, even if they are wholly owned. Moreover, firms with expertise in manufacturing may not have similar expertise in retailing. Finally, economies of scope in retailing may mean that it is best for retailers to carry many other products in addition to one manufacturer's particular product.

Together, these facts mean that a manufacturer who wants to control the behavior of retailers so that they will behave in certain ways must establish a set of incentives which make it in the interest of the retailer to do what the manufacturer wants. The manufacturer cannot in general specify this behavior through contract, nor can be necessarily own the retailer and use direct hierarchial control. He is thus faced with the familiar problem of designing a set of *implicit contracts* which will provide appropriate incentives.

This chapter should be useful for two purposes. For manufacturers, it will indicate the sorts of restrictions they should place on retailers. It can provide suggestions as to valuable types of behavior manufacturers may want from retailers, and ways of eliciting this behavior. For retail firms, the chapter will indicate the ways in which they might contract so as to make their services more valuable to suppliers, who will then be willing to pay them more or allocate greater volume. As always, efficient contracts can increase value for both parties.

WHY MANUFACTURERS IMPOSE RESTRICTIONS

One option for manufacturers is simply to sell their product at a given wholesale price to all comers and not to worry about what happens after this sale. The advantage of this procedure should be familiar by now: It makes use of market incentives, and these incentives are very powerful. Once a manufacturer has picked a wholesale price, he wants the retail price to be as low as possible because this will maximize sales to consumers. Thus, it is in the manufacturer's interest to keep distribution costs as low as possible. Unrestricted sale to all comers will force all retailers to compete and this will generate exactly the sort of pressures for low cost and low profits at the retail level which should be in the manufacturer's interest. Indeed, some producers do engage in just this sort of pricing and marketing behavior. Producers who do not brand or label their products are particularly unlikely to place any additional restrictions on retailers.

But many producers do impose various restrictions and conditions on firms selling their products. Indeed, most manufacturers who brand their products probably place additional restrictions at the retail level. Moreover, such restrictions have costs. These costs may be direct, such as the costs of providing demonstrations, or indirect, as when limiting the number of retailers in an area enables each to charge a somewhat higher price. Since there are costs to the producer of restricting behavior, there must be offsetting benefits in terms of increased demand, leading to increased sales or prices. There are many services which retailers can provide which increase the demand for the product by enough to compensate for the costs of the restrictions. Some of these are described below.

Before turning to a description of dealer-supplied services, however, a general point is in order. We must ask why manufacturers want higher levels of services than retailers or dealers want to provide. The general answer is in terms of a type of shirking which we have not yet seen, *free riding*. Free riding is earning profits on the efforts of others. (For an example, from franchising, if one McDonald's were to offer low quality it would still get sales because many consumers would perceive it as being the same as other McDonald's, at least until they had eaten, when it would be too late. The low-quality restaurant would be free riding on the level of quality provided by others.)

In a situation where party A can free ride on the investment of party B, it will soon pay B to stop providing the service. (If the quality deterioration in McDonald's were to become widespread, then no McDonald's would invest in providing quality.) If the service increases sales and manufacturer profits, then free riding will harm manufacturers. If consumers value the service, then free riding will ultimately harm consumers. In the sort of situations discussed in this chapter, free riding will generally harm both manufacturers and consumers.

For each of the types of services manufacturers want provided, there are possibilities of free riding. The free riding may be with respect to the efforts of the manufacturer itself or with respect to efforts of other dealers. This means that, unless contractual devices can be used to align dealer and manufacturer incentives, less of these services than manufacturers want will be provided. At this point, many of the services, and the sorts of free riding associated with each, will be discussed, along with the contractual mechanisms available for controlling free riding in each of the cases considered.

WHAT DO MANUFACTURERS WANT?

In this section I will discuss many of the services which manufacturers want dealers to provide, and why dealers, if left to their own devices, would not provide enough of these services. In reading this section, you should consider characteristics of products you sell to determine if sales could be increased if any of these services were provided. If so, the next section will indicate ways of inducing dealers to provide them.

Demonstration of the Product

Consider a product such as a stereo speaker. This product may be complex, and consumers may be unwilling to buy it without a demonstration. For a speaker, for example, the demonstration should be done in a sound room. It is in manufacturers' interests to have retailers provide such a facility. Similar analyses would apply to any complex product where sales are increased by the provision of expensive demonstration services, or even by the mere display of the product.

Here, however, dealers can free ride on services provided by other dealers. If dealer A provides a sound room, this will be costly. The price charged by A will have to be large enough to compensate for the service. Dealer B would like to have an option of advertising, "Go to A and listen to the speakers. Decide which you want, and then order from us at 10 percent off." B could do this because he has saved the cost of the demonstration. However, if many customers listened at A and bought at B, then Dealer A would find that he could not support the provision of the sound room, and would cease doing so. This would harm the producer (who would lose sales because of the lack of a sound room) and also consumers, who would ultimately be deprived of the ability to listen before buying. It is in the interests of manufacturers to devise ways of preventing B's free-riding behavior. (It is also in the long-run interests of consumers to prevent it, but of course in the short run any given consumer will have an incentive to shop at B and save the 10 percent. Consumers will also free ride.)

Quality Certification

Consider a good such as a fashion dress. Consumers may not know which styles are in fashion this year, and this information is valuable to some consumers. Certain stores may specialize in studying fashion markets and learning which goods are currently in style. A manufacturer may want his goods displayed in these stores. This can indicate to consumers that this brand is indeed in vogue *right now!* A similar analysis can apply in general to any dimension of quality. Buyers in some stores may spend resources testing products and then carry only high-quality products. In this case, the fact that a certain store carries a brand is valuable information to consumers.

Free riding in this case is obvious. If it could, Xmart, the discount outlet, can send its buyers to HighStyle, the fashion store, and see what it is carrying. Sending a buyer to HighStyle is cheaper than market research and testing, so that it is cheaper for Xmart to inspect HighStyle than to do its own testing. Xmart can then offer the same product at a lower price because it has not spent money in learning about product characteristics. Consumers go to HighStyle, observe what is being carried, and buy at Xmart. However, HighStyle will soon cease spending resources on learning and testing if it cannot sell any merchandise at the premium price required to compensate it for its spending. Again, as a result, manufacturers lose because less is sold and consumers lose because the information they want is not produced.

Maintainence of Freshness

Some goods deteriorate with age or with certain kinds of storage (e.g., lack of refrigeration). Manufacturers may want retailers to rotate stocks to eliminate stale goods, or to maintain refrigeration in order to prevent deterioration. If there were no controls, there are two kinds of free riding which could be associated with these goods.

First, if consumers bought stale or spoiled versions of the good, they might associate the low quality with the brand, rather than with the retailer, and stop buying this brand rather than switching retailers. Part of the loss would be borne by the retailer, who would lose sales in the future, but part would be borne by the manufacturer. In fact, if consumers switched to other brands, the retailer might not feel any effect. Therefore, the retailer, who would bear at most only a fraction of the cost, would underinvest in maintaining freshness.

There could also be free riding with respect to other retailers. For many goods, consumers shop in different outlets and may not know which particular loaf of bread was bought at Safeway and which at 7–11. Therefore, if one retailer sells stale goods, consumers may again reduce their purchases from both stores, and both retailers may suffer.

Promotional Efforts for Marginal Consumers

Manufacturers may want retailers to spend particular efforts demonstrating products to consumers who are on the margin of buying the product; such promotions may require specialized personnel dedicated to demonstrating the particular product. This will happen in the following circumstances. First, the manufacturers' profits on the item must be greater than the retailers' profits. Second, there must be some marginal consumers who need more sales effort to be induced to buy than does the average consumer. (If all consumers were the same in this regard, retailers would increase spending on promotions and increase price to compensate to the point where profits were maximized.) However, if consumers differ, then it is in manufacturers' interests to have retailers spend more on promotion than may be in retailers' interests.

Service in the Store

Manufacturers may want stores to give particularly prominent locations or large amounts of shelf space to their products. They may also want additional sales people or highly trained sales people to sell their products. They may want these services on a regular basis, or in connection with particular advertising or promotional campaigns. If manufacturer profits per unit are greater than retailer profits, then retailers may not want to give products the same prominence as producers want. We will see below how this can lead to free riding.

Inventories

Manufacturers may want dealers to carry full, complete inventories of products. It may be in the interests of dealers to carry only those products (e.g., sizes or colors) which sell best. A dealer carrying an incomplete line can then free ride on dealers carrying complete lines. Since carrying a large inventory will be costly, the dealer carrying the partial line can sell at a lower price. However, this means that the full-line dealer will not be able to sell enough to compensate for carrying the full line, and will stop. Again, manufacturers will lose as dealers stop carrying the full line, and consumer will lose as they are unable to buy odd sizes or colors.

Number of Dealers

In some cases, manufacturers may want a larger number of dealers than would be generated through normal market forces. There are several advantages to this practice. Having many dealers may serve to reinforce the name of the product in the consumer's mind, and thus be a promotional device. Multiple dealers may increase competition among dealers, and thus sales of the product. By having several dealers in a market, a manufacturer may have some measure of expected performance, and thus be able to monitor dealer effort. It will also be possible to set up "contests" (payment schemes based on relative performance, discussed in detail in Chapter 3) if there are several dealers. However, if there are economies of scale in selling, the natural market equilibrium may end up with too few dealers (from the producer's perspective). This situation is perhaps characteristic of the auto industry.

Type of Dealer

Manufacturers may want their products carried only in "prestige" stores because sale in discount outlets may reduce the value of the brand name. However, if left to their own devices, wholesalers may sell some units to discounters, or some retailers may transship extra units. If consumers lose their perception of the brand as being carried only in "exclusive" shops, total sales may decrease. The product is valuable to the discounter precisely because of its prestige reputation, but sale in discount stores will quickly erode this reputation.

Undesirable Dealer Behavior

Manufacturers may want retailers to refrain from certain kinds of behavior, and in particular from switching consumers to other lines. For instance, a manufacturer has advertised product A, and the price of A must reflect this advertising, so that it is higher than the price of B. This means that the dealer may make a larger profit on B than on A. A consumer learns of the product through advertising and comes into the store and asks for A. The retailer may have an incentive to try to convince the consumer that B is just as good, or a better buy. Manufacturers obviously do not want retailers to do this. Moreover, if dealers do behave in this way, manufacturers will reduce their advertising, and there will be the standard loss in consumer and producer welfare.

INCENTIVES

Consider the following: If a dealer shirks or free rides, he will make a profit in the ways described above. He will either sell more or reduce his costs by his shirking. Ultimately, the manufacturer will detect this shirking and punish the dealer. Since it is impossible to contractually specify the behavior of retailers, there will be no possibility of the producer suing for damages caused by the shirking. All contracts discussed in this chapter are "implicit" and do not lead to the possibility of litigation for damages. The only remedy available to the producer for punishing the dealer is termination of the relationship. Since they are implicit, the contracts considered in this chapter are "self-enforcing."

The situation facing the dealer is then this: By shirking he will make profits in the short run, the period until he is caught. In the long run, he will lose whatever benefits there are from dealing with this particular manufacturer. Therefore, the dealer, in deciding whether or not to shirk, will balance the short-run gains from cheating against the long-run costs. The producer, knowing that this is the intent of the retailer, must try to increase the long-run costs of cheating and reduce the short-run benefits.

The downside to the retailer of being caught shirking is the loss of future business with the producer. However, unless the retailer is earning some profits on sales of the product, there is no cost from loss of the business. That is, if the producer is just earning a normal return on his business with the manufacturer, then any positive profits from cheating will be sufficient to cause cheating to be worthwhile. Therefore, the first principle is that the dealer must make some positive returns on the business.

This return need not be actual profits; it may be in the form of a quasirent (that is, a return on a fixed investment). For example, a producer may require a retailer to build expensive display racks in his store in order to be allowed to carry the line of the producer. Then any return on the investment in these racks will be a quasirent. However, any loss of the business will lead to a reduction in the value of the investment. Therefore, the dealer will not want to lose this business. For some cases, there may be no possibility of the manufacturer forcing the dealer to invest in such capital. In these cases, it will still be necessary for the dealer to earn a profit for the mechanisms discussed to operate; there must be something valuable which the dealer will lose from termination. In what follows, I will refer to lost quasirents, but you should remember that this may be actual profits (rents) or quasirents.

A second issue is the length of the "short run." In this context, the short run is defined as that period during which cheating can occur, before the cheater is caught. Therefore, the length of the short run is determined by the efforts at monitoring by the producer. If more is spent on monitoring, then the short run is shorter (shirkers will be detected sooner). If less is spent, then free riding can go on for a longer time. The larger the quasirents associated with the product are, the less that must be spent on monitoring, because the expected value of cheating will fall as quasirents increase. There is a tradeoff: Larger profits or quasirents earned by the dealer require lower spending on monitoring by the manufacturer.

One option available to the producer to generate quasirents would be the use of a two-part tariff, as discussed in Chapter 3. The producer charges the retailer a fixed amount for the right to carry the product. The producer can then lower the wholesale price since he has earned some returns through the fixed charge, and the retailer can make a return on this fixed charge through his markup. In the limit, this scheme could be used to allocate *all* of the quasirents associated with the product to the retailer in return for the upfront fixed payment. However, this would create a problem of cheating on the part of the producer. If the manufacturer earned no profits from the product, then he would have no incentive to maintain quality. Thus, there is a limit to the amount of quasirent which can be transferred. Nonetheless, managers should be aware of the possibility of using some fixed payments coupled with reduced prices for minimization of agency problems. (As discussed in detail in the next chapter, a franchise fee is an example of such a payment scheme.)

Sometimes the opposite occurs, and retailers occasionally charge manufacturers for space for sale of products. This is particularly common in food stores, where the retailer may charge for "shelf space." The practice is most common for new products, and may best be viewed as a mechanism for forcing manufacturers to pretest their products. A manufacturer will only invest in payments for shelf space for products which it expects to do well. By requiring a payment, retailers are able to shift the costs of pretesting to producers, who are best able to perform such testing.

If there are competing dealers (perhaps in different regions under an exclusive territory allocation scheme) manufacturers have an additional option. They can rely on a "contest," as discussed in Chapter 3. That is, manufacturers can allow each dealer to earn profits based on sales of the dealership, but couple this mechanism with a bonus for the dealer with the largest sales. This will be an efficient device if sales across regions are correlated and associated with some unobservable variable, such as consumer demand for the product. It will also be possible if there are several dealers in a region, which may be a reason for manufacturers preferring more dealers than would be provided by the market, as discussed above. In either of these cases, as indicated in Chapter 3, a contest can both increase incentives and reduce risk.

We now have three pieces to the puzzle. We have a list of mechanisms available to manufacturers, a list of goals, and a list of forms of free riding. How can we relate the mechanisms discussed in the first part of this chapter to the goals of manufacturers and the possible types of free riding discussed above? Let us consider each mechanism and show the goals it achieves.

Minimum Price Restrictions (Resale Price Maintenance, RPM)

This is the most controversial mechanism used by producers, but it is the most powerful and perhaps the easiest to understand. A minimum price means that each unit sold by a retailer brings in a certain amount of profit. This is the ultimate source of quasirents. If a dealer cheats on some aspect of the agreement (as by not providing demonstration facilities, or not preserving the freshness of the product), then when the cheating is detected the retailer loses the quasirents associated with the high price from sales it would otherwise have obtained in the future. Thus, resale price maintenance increases the long-run cost of shirking.

Moreover, many forms of retailer cheating lead to reduced costs. Reduced costs are more valuable to a firm if they are passed on to consumers through reduced prices because they lead to an increase in sales. However, a requirement of minimum prices means that there are limits to gains from cost-reducing cheating because shirking retailers cannot pass on the reduced costs through price decreases. Of course, firms might further cheat by reducing prices below the minimum. However, this form of cheating would be exceptionally easy to detect (since it would be valuable only if advertised and since competitive retailers would help the manufacturer in policing) and therefore would be unlikely. Thus, minimum prices work in two ways to reduce cheating. They increase the long-run costs of free riding by increasing the future quasirents to be obtained if the relationship between the dealer and the producer continues. They also reduce the gains from cheating because they reduce the increase in sales which might occur from reduced costs, as they limit the ability of the shirker to increase sales by reducing retail prices.

Since it is an efficient method of generating quasirents, resale price maintenance is useful for performing most of the functions mentioned above. We have already indicated ways in which RPM reduces incentives for shirking on demonstration services and on maintaining freshness. It also facilitates quality certification. By maintaining a minimum price, those outlets which test and certify the product will be compensated. Gains to discounters would be reduced since they could not compete by lowering price. Similarly, higher retail prices will be a way of compensating retailers for promotional efforts aimed at marginal consumers. The higher price is a way of compensating dealers for offering services to marginal consumers which might not be in the interests of the dealers (since producer profits per unit are greater then dealer profits). Those dealers who sell at lower prices are free riding on these promotional efforts, since the higher price is a form of compensation for offering the higher level of services. These fixed retail prices may also be a method of compensating dealers for carrying full inventories, and for providing prominent locations or additional services in stores.

Exclusive Territories

This device is the closest substitute for resale price maintenance. If a seller has an exclusive territory, then it can earn higher returns in that territory because there is reduced competition. Therefore, such territories are associated with positive quasirents. They can be used as an alternative to RPM where the latter is illegal, and can therefore perform most of the functions of RPM. Exclusive territories can work in two ways. At the wholesale level, customers may be allocated to dealers, and wholesalers may be forbidden from selling to customers of other wholesalers. This is impossible at the retail level, and at this level the only option is a territorial restriction.

Exclusive territories can lead to prices which are too high from the perspective of the producer if the exclusivity gives the retailer a monopoly position within the territory. This will lead to inefficiently low sales (from the perspective of both the manufacturer and consumers). Therefore, this form of vertical restriction is often associated with maximum retail prices, where such restrictions are legal. An alternative is a quota, requiring that each retailer take a certain amount of product, where the quota would depend on expected sales in the territory. Manufacturers can also monitor dealer sales and penalize (perhaps by cancellation) any dealer who does not sell enough of the product. These mechanisms reduce the gains from possession of an exclusive territory and enable the producer to better tailor the profits of the retailer to achieve the goals of the producer.

There are other benefits from exclusive territories, associated with various forms of interdealer free riding. For example, if there is only one dealer in a territory, then there are reduced incentives for free riding on dealer-supplied demonstrations. Similarly, a single dealer will have incentives to provide the optimal amount of freshness, since the sole distributor will lose all sales which are lost in a territory as a result of selling stale product. A single dealer will also carry a complete inventory.

The main threat to exclusive territories may be mail order sales from outside of the territory. Mail order firms are particularly likely to free ride on dealer-provided services, such as demonstrations. A related problem has recently occurred with imported goods, where exclusive U.S. importing agents of certain products (e.g., Japanese cameras) may provide warranty repair work for products which have been imported into the United States by other means.

Exclusive Dealing

This is a restriction that allows retailers to carry only the product of a particular manufacturer. (A similar restriction is a "requirements contract," a contract which specifies that a retailer must obtain all of his requirements of a particular input only from one producer.) It is aimed at preventing retailers from shifting consumers from the product of the manufacturer to other products which may be cheaper or more profitable for the retailer. It will be particularly useful in those circumstances where producers have spent resources (as in advertising) to generate business for retailers. A retailer may be required to carry only one product (in which case it is likely to be a franchise, discussed in the next chapter), or only one version of a particular product if the industry is one in which retailers generally carry a large line of products.

Consider the following: A producer has spent substantial amounts generating business for a product. This advertising and promotion is best suited to induce consumers to go to a retail establishment to test the product. Because of this expensive promotion, the product is more costly than similar products, but the information about the product provided in advertising is valuable to consumers.

There are complimentary services provided by the retailer, such as demonstrations and instruction. The manufacturer wants to be sure that the retailer is providing the desired level of services. One method of monitoring is to measure sales in the territory, and assume shirking if sales are too low. (Creation of additional dealerships in a territory may sometimes facilitate such monitoring because comparisons become easier, but this will lose the advantages of exclusive territories.) However, there will be some uncertainty about sales, and low levels may be due to random factors (although manufacturers will often attempt to measure dealer performance based on sales). Another option is direct monitoring of dealer efforts. For example, the manufacturer may require that the dealer have a certain number of salespeople for the product, and that they be highly trained. But the dealer might use these sales personnel to sell products of another manufacturer if these are more profitable (because, for example the other manufacturer has not spent much on advertising). In this case, exclusive dealing (forbidding the dealer from carrying any other brands) will be an efficient response.

Maximum Purchase Requirements

When the producer desires more retailers than natural market forces would generate, then a restriction on the amount of product each dealer can sell may be efficient. This restriction may apply to the auto industry, where economies of scale would lead to fewer dealers and larger dealers than producers would desire. Resale price maintenance would not be a solution in this industry because of the extensive bargaining over selling price for new cars and over price paid for a trade-in. Because cars are expensive, consumers would be willing to travel long distances for purchase, so that there would be difficulties in establishing exclusive territories for distribution. Therefore, dealers are allocated cars to sell based on past sales and other factors. Since the volume of cars available from competitors is limited by this quota, each dealer can earn quasirents, but there are more dealers than would occur in an unaided equilibrium.

Producer Provision of Services

Some manufacturers will themselves directly provide some services to consumers. One example is the hiring of sales personnel to sell cosmetics and perfume in department stores; these personnel are hired by the manufacturer rather than by the retailer. The manufacturer would want the retailer to spend a certain amount on promotional efforts, and compensates the retailer through the quasirent stream. However, there are strong incentives for the retailer to shirk by having these personnel sell other lines which may be even higher profit (because they have not spent as much on advertising and promotion). If these incentives are too strong, then the most efficient method of enforcement for the manufacturer may be the direct hiring of the personnel, rather than relying on monitoring to detect cheating by the retailer's employees.

Sometimes manufacturers will advertise directly in a region. Often advertising will be "cooperative," in that both the producer and the retailer will pay for the ads. This is particularly common when the ad names both the product and the retail establishment. In this case, some of the benefits of the ad go to other customers of the retail establishment, and some go to other stores selling the product. (The ad says, "Get your Widgets at Smith's." Some consumers will buy Widgets at Jones's, and some will buy Gadgets at Smith's.) Therefore, neither party would have incentives to spend the efficient amount on advertising. Cooperative advertising can overcome this inefficiency.

Tying

There is an additional form of vertical control called "tying," which is a requirement that two products be purchased together. This type of control can serve several functions.* Note, however, that tying is an issue only in special circumstances. In the general case, if there are complimentarities between two products, they will be sold together. (Tires are not tied to cars; rather, the automobile manufacturer chooses the best set of tires for the car and sells them together.) Tying may occur where one input is fixed and the other variable, so that they cannot be bundled. A classic example is the use of IBM punch cards and IBM computers, discussed below. Another example was the requirement (since abolished) that consumers return automobiles to the original dealership for maintenance in order to maintain the warranty. In general, however, if there are reasons for selling two products together, the easiest way to do so is to make them into one product. Tying only occurs when this cannot be accomplished.

Often there is technological interdependence between two products. In this case, product A will function better if it is used with product B. While it is in the interests of both buyers and sellers for A to function well, buyers may not have the information needed to determine the relationship. Moreover, the seller's reputation may suffer if a low-quality version of B is used with A and therefore A malfunctions. A requirement that both products be purchased together will then guarantee the quality of each.

A second use of tying is as a metering device. This was probably involved in the IBM matter. Since the value of a computer can vary from consumer to consumer, IBM, given that it had some market power in the computer market, would like to have charged on the basis of this value. Thus, charging a fixed rental for a computer and an additional price for punch cards will accomplish this, as the use of cards is likely to be associated with value to the consumer. Note that this does not create any monopoly power. It merely enables a firm to use what monopoly power it may have more effectively. It will also serve to increase total sales (since the alternative is a single price to all consumers which will reduce sales to some consumers) and therefore increase consumer welfare.

SUMMARY

Manufacturers often want to control the behavior of retailers in various ways. There are possibilities for shirking by retailers; most of

* As before, the reader should note that there are serious but misguided antitrust issues raised by tying contracts.

132   *Managing Business Transactions*

these take the form of free riding. This free riding may be on invest-ments of the manufacturer or of other retailers. Some of the services which manufacturers may want performed by retailers are: demonstrat-ing the product, certifying quality, maintaining freshness, providing promotional efforts, providing prominent displays and other in-store service, and maintaining complete inventories. Manufacturers may also have an interest in the number and type of dealers for their products. Finally, there are certain behaviors which manufacturers want to pre-vent on the part of dealers, including switching consumers to other products.

In order to achieve these goals, there are several mechanisms available to producers. The goal of these mechanisms is to reduce the short-run gains from dealer cheating and to increase the long-run costs. For cheating to be costly, dealers must earn quasirents on the manufac-turers' products which they sell. If there are no quasirents, retailers have nothing to lose from cheating and so cannot be deterred. Therefore, the available mechanisms can either increase these quasirents or reduce gains from cheating. One possibility is charging a fee and giving the retailer most of all of the quasirents associated with the product, but this is of limited use because it gives manufacturers an incentive to cheat on quality. Some of the other mechanisms available are: resale price main-tenance; exclusive territories, commonly coupled with minimum sales quotas or maximum resale prices; exclusive dealing, requiring that the dealer carry only the brand of the manufacturer; and maximum pur-chase requirements. Producers will sometimes provide services to consumers directly at the point of purchase. Finally, manufacturers will often tie the purchase of two products, either to improve quality or to meter and charge for differing demands.

The relations between product characteristics, desired retailer behaviors, and mechanisms available to achieve these behaviors is complex. This chapter has indicated the nature of some of these rela-tionships. For a manager of a manufacturing firm, the chapter should indicate the kinds of things to look for in designing contracts or terms of trade with retailers. For a retailer, the chapter should indicate the kinds of deals it can offer to get more business from suppliers.

REFERENCES

Blair, Roger D. and Kaserman, David L. *Antitrust Economics,* Chapters 13–16. Home-wood, Ill.: Richard D. Irwin. 1985.

Katz, Michael L. "Vertical Contractual Relations." In *Handbook of Industrial Organization,* edited by Richard Schmalensee and Robert Willig.

Klein, Benjamin, and Murphy, Kevin M. "Vertical Restraints as Contract Enforcement Mechanisms." *Journal of Law and Economics* 31 (1988):265.

Marvel, Howard P. "Exclusive Dealing." *Journal of Law and Economics* 25 (1982):1.

Marvel, Howard P., and McCafferty, Stephen. "Resale Price Maintenance and Quality Certification." *Rand Journal of Economics* 15 (1984):346.

Mathewson, G. Frank, and Winter, Ralph A. "An Economic Theory of Vertical Restraints." *Rand Journal of Economics* 15 (1984):27.

Telser, Lester G. "Why Should Manufacturers Want Fair Trade?" *Journal of Law and Economics* 3 (1960):86.

– 7 –

Franchising

In the last chapter, we discussed vertical controls which a firm might find worth installing in order to guarantee that distributors will provide correct amounts of services for buyers of the product. An alternative is to maintain distributors selling only the product of the firm. Such distributors can be wholly owned or franchised. In this chapter, we cover the advantages and disadvantages of franchising, and the structure of the relationship between the firm and its franchisees if that strategy is chosen.

Franchising is a particular example of a more general method of allocating rights and responsibilities. Party A owns some rights which would be valuable to party B. The value of the rights depends on actions by both A and B. Then the payment from B to A for the rights will be in the form of an upfront cash payment plus a variable payment linked to output. The structure of the payments depends on both the actions which each party can take and the risk preferences of each. For example, if B pays the entire expected value of the earnings stream up front, then B bears the entire risk associated with the use of the right. Moreover, if B pays the entire amount, then A will not undertake any actions which he controls to maximize value. On the other hand, this scheme will reduce shirking by B since he bears the entire cost of any shirking. In this chapter, we will see the exact workings of such a scheme in the context of franchising, but the same issues arise in many compensation schemes.

FRANCHISE OR OWNERSHIP: NOT CAPITAL

Once a firm has decided to establish its own retail outlets, the next question is whether these outlets should be owned by the firm or

134

independently owned. Independent ownership means that the outlets will be franchises.

Perhaps the most important point to note is that a common explanation for franchising—raising capital—is simply wrong. It is often said that firms use franchising because they lack the capital needed to finance expansion on their own. If a successful businessman is planning to expand, he must decide whether to do this by franchising or by direct ownership of additional businesses. Such a businessman will be misled if he makes this decision on the basis of capital.

Consider a firm that already has an equity position in a successful business—say, a restaurant specializing in broiled chicken. (If there were no successful outlet, the issue would never arise.) It now needs additional capital (say, $200,000) in order to start another store. One way to get this equity is to offer a franchise to a new owner of the new store, and require the franchisee to put up the $200,000. If this strategy is chosen and the new store is successful, the franchisee will ultimately own one-half of the assets of the company since he will own one of two stores.

This new store is risky. It is riskier than the existing store since that one is already operating successfully. The potential franchisee knows about this risk. Lenders and owners of capital dislike risk, and need to be compensated for bearing it. Therefore, if the business is financed by a franchisee he is going to demand a greater level of compensation if he is required to make a riskier investment. A greater level of compensation for the franchisee ultimately means less for the franchisor. Therefore, if the franchisor can reduce the risk he can ultimately benefit. This is a corollary of the point that efficient contracts benefit all parties.

In general, the way to manage risk is to diversify as much as possible. In the situation here, the established restaurant is relatively safe, and the potential new restaurant is relatively risky. If a franchise is the method chosen, the franchisee has a portfolio of only one establishment, the risky one. The founder has a portfolio of only one restaurant, the less risky one. This set of investment portfolios is riskier than a set of portfolios made up of fractions of each store. Consider instead the following option: Establish a business entity which will own both stores, and offer to sell shares in this entity. Remember that $200,000 is needed to establish the new enterprise. How much of the stock in the joint enterprise will need to be sold in order to raise $200,000? The answer is: considerably less than half. Because the investor is getting a much less risky investment for his money, he will therefore require a much smaller share in order to make the investment.

Of course, the original owner is now bearing some of the risk. However, if he does not want to do so, he can eliminate the risk. For example, one option is to sell half of the enterprise. This is what would have occurred if the franchise route were taken. However, since there is less risk, it is now possible to get more than $200,000 for the 50 percent interest in the combination of two restaurants. The original owner can take the difference and pocket it, thus reducing his risk as well. While the math is complicated, it can be shown that by diversifying the risk into a portfolio, all investors in the process can gain; or, what is the same thing, the cost of capital to the original founder can be reduced.

There is another benefit from this sort of diversification. If the franchise route is chosen, then the person who invests in the franchise must also operate the restaurant. By restricting potential investors to those persons with an interest in operating a restaurant, the founder is reducing his pool of investors and therefore again increasing his cost of capital. If the investment route is taken, then anyone with sufficient capital becomes a potential investor.

The point is clear: If the only reason why a founder is considering using a franchise for expansion is a lack of capital, then he should not use franchising. Sale of shares in an entity owning part of old and new stores is a more efficient way to raise capital. Franchising is only justified if there is some other, noncapital benefit. In many cases, there are such benefits.

FRANCHISE OR OWNERSHIP: EFFICIENCY DIFFERENCES

The argument so far has implicitly assumed that the new entity will be equally profitable if it is run by the founder or by the franchisee. We must now examine this assumption because this, not the capital argument, is the real key to the franchise-or-own issue. The key benefit from franchising is the creation of proper incentives, whereas the major cost of franchising is the loss of control. The issue of franchised versus owned outlets is therefore the tradeoff between the improved incentives associated with franchising versus the improved control associated with ownership. As we will see, this tradeoff is complex.

First consider incentives. A franchise is generally a retail establishment. For such an establishment, there are numerous details which determine profitability. Many of these details are associated with the day-to-day operation of the business. For example, in a restaurant, the most familiar type of franchise, these details largely deal with employee supervision. In order to make a profit in a restaurant, it is necessary to closely supervise the workforce because the workers are generally not career oriented, the tasks are unpleasant and repetitive, and the costs to the owner of employee shirking are substantial as measured in waste, theft, or lost future business. Such supervision requires close monitoring by a motivated manager. For these reasons, most restaurants are owner managed. (Note that this monitoring has to do with how hard employees work, something which it will be difficult for a customer to determine. It does not involve monitoring of quality of the product or necessarily of service.)

How does one motivate a manager? One way is to measure output (the profitability of the business) and reward the manager accordingly. However, this is difficult to do in a franchise context. Determinants of profitability are complex, and there is a large random element involved. Therefore, using observed profits as a guide to managerial effort will create a large random element. People must be paid for bearing risk, so managers who know that their incomes are subject to large random fluctuations will demand higher salaries to compensate, and this will raise the costs of doing business and reduce profits.

If the manager is also the owner, then the incentives are correct. That is, if the outlet is run by someone who gets all of the profits, as does an owner, then there is a proper incentive for efficient operation. A franchise is exactly such an endeavor: The manager of the outlet is the owner and has residual rights in all the profits, so that there is an incentive for efficient operation. This improvement in incentives for efficient management is the ultimate gain from franchising.

There is, however, a cost. To see this, it is useful to consider the structure of a franchised business, such as McDonald's. McDonald's sells hamburgers. However, this is not why the firm is so successful. Rather, what McDonald's is really selling is hamburgers with a low variance in quality. The advantage of patronizing McDonald's rather than another hamburger restaurant is the certainty involved: When I take my family into McDonald's (or the other major franchised restaurant chains) I know what I am going to get, whether the outlet is in Montana or Manhattan or, now, in Moscow. The provision of this certainty is why franchised chains prosper.

But think of the incentives created. For any given McDonald's, part of its sales comes about exactly because of the certainty associated with the system, not with the particular restaurant. For a particular store, some of the customers have never eaten there before and will never eat there again. For these customers, actual quality in this store is irrelevant because it is not observed until after the transaction is complete. Therefore, if the owner or manager of a restaurant can save money by reducing quality, he can increase profits. But this profit for the owner of a particular restaurant is purchased at the expense of all the other outlets in the chain, since customers who obtain low quality at a single McDonald's are less likely to patronize any other member of the chain. (In technical economic jargon, we say that quality in one outlet creates an *externality* for other outlets, or that there is an incentive for owners to free ride on quality produced by other stores.) For McDonald's as a franchisor, it is important to control the quality offered by each outlet in the chain because this will maximize the value of the entire chain.

This is the benefit of central ownership. For a centrally owned restaurant, the manager of a particular store has no incentive to reduce quality since he does not get the profits associated with this quality reduction. On the other hand, since he does not get the profits associated with maintaining labor productivity, the manager who is not an owner has a reduced incentive to supervise the outlet efficiently. This is the tradeoff between incentives (for efficient management) and control (over quality) which goes into the own-or-franchise decision.

One important element in deciding on ownership form is geography. If the owner of the trademark is considering opening a new store near his present store, then ownership is relatively more desirable. This is because it may be possible for the owner to effectively monitor both stores for productivity. Moreover, if stores are near each other, then sales will be affected by common factors, and a contest may be an efficient tool for monitoring and rewarding performance of managers. Similarly, if there are several stores near each other, it may be useful for them to all be owned and monitored by a company employee. It will be possible to measure the performance of this employee since chance events should balance out if he is supervising many stores, and he can be rewarded on the basis of the profitability of the group of stores. On the other hand, for a single, isolated store local ownership is relatively more desirable, since efficient monitoring is difficult for such a store. The best strategy may be to establish franchises in distant locations with the plan of acquiring them when and if enough stores come to being in a particular location to make hiring a manager feasible. Contracts should be written with this end in mind. For example, many contracts in a given region might be written with a common termination date. Of course, for a franchise, quality monitoring must still occur.

FRANCHISOR-FRANCHISEE RELATIONSHIPS: REVENUES

The franchisor has something valuable to sell. Generally, this is a product or marketing system and the associated trademark. Using the considerations discussed above, it has been decided that the best way to profit from this item is through franchising of at least some dealers. There are three ways to earn revenues from a franchised outlet: the franchise fee, royalties as a percentage of sales, and profits on goods sold by the franchisor to the franchisee.* The amount of profits which should be earned from each source is related to incentives. A franchise agreement is an example of the sort of two-part payment schedule discussed in Chapter 3.

First note that both the franchisee and the franchisor want the joint profits to be as large as possible. Since they are contracting with each other, it is easy for them to devise mechanisms for splitting these profits. Therefore, the goal should be to have as large a pie as possible to split. Any mechanism which raises franchisor revenues by some amount but lowers franchisee revenues by more should be avoided, for there is always some alternative which is better. Efficient contracts are to be preferred.

If revenues are earned as royalties on sales or profits on inputs, then incentives for efficient franchise operation is reduced. Recall that the rationale for franchising was to give franchises incentives to manage the store efficiently by making them residual claimants. Any reduction in the return for efficient management, such as a royalty on sales or a higher cost of inputs, reduces this incentive and thus reduces the incentive for efficient management. On the other hand, revenues earned from the franchise fee are efficient with respect to the franchisee. The fee is a fixed payment and does not depend on sales or profits. Therefore, it does not reduce the incentive of the franchisee to police the efficient operation of the business. From the perspective of franchisee efficiency, we would expect the fixed fee to be as large as

---

*A note of caution: Antitrust laws sometimes make it difficult to require direct purchase from the franchisor. However, the law is fluid in this area and as of now seems to be quickly evolving towards a more rational attitude which would allow requiring direct purchase. This is a case where it is important to get legal advice from a competent antitrust practitioner before drafting contracts. However, it is equally important to explain to the lawyer exactly what you want to accomplish since that will enable him to draw up the best contract for your needs. In what follows I will ignore antitrust restrictions and discuss only management goals.

possible and the royalty payments to the franchisor to be as small as possible. In other words, we would expect the franchisor to make as much of his return as possible from the fee, and as little as possible from royalties.

How large is this? Consider a franchise which will generate, say, $100,000 in total annual gains to the franchisee. Assume that franchisees must be competent restaurant managers who could earn $60,000 in salary working for someone else. Then the franchise is worth $40,000 per year to the franchisee. The present value of $40,000 over e.g., a ten-year period at 10 percent interest is about $250,000. If the franchise contract is for ten years, then the franchise fee should be, as a first approximation, about $250,000. In other words, the fee should be approximately the amount which will just make the franchisee indifferent between buying the franchise and working at his next best alternative.

However, there is a cost to letting the franchisor gain all of his revenue from the fee. We have so far discussed franchisee shirking, but there is also a possibility of franchisor shirking. There are various tasks which the franchisor should perform, and the contract should provide proper incentives for performing these tasks. If the contract does this, then the value of the franchise will be greater and the franchisees will pay more for their rights. Therefore, the franchisor will try to write as efficient a set of contracts as possible, and this will include giving the franchisor efficient incentives.

For one example, all franchisees expect the franchisor to invest in policing the quality of the chain. This is because such policing is necessary to maximize the value of the franchise. If the franchisor makes his entire revenue from franchise fees, however, then he will have no incentive to continue policing once the franchise system stops growing. Therefore, some of the profits of the franchisor should come from ongoing revenues earned from franchisees in order to give the franchisor correct incentives. Franchisees will perceive these incentives and therefore will be willing to pay more for the franchise rights in total if they know that policing will continue. As a result, at least part of the return to the franchisor should be in the form of royalties.

A royalty on sales treats all sales of all products as identical. To the extent that different products sold by the franchise generate different levels of profit for the franchisor, or are associated with different levels of costs, it is more desirable to earn profits on sales to franchisees because such earnings can vary over products. For example, if a franchisor is developing and advertising heavily a new product, then he should earn profits on this product by requiring the franchisee to purchase it from him. The franchisor can structure the terms so that he earns a relatively large profit on this item, perhaps to compensate for the advertising costs. It is possible to vary profits over products if the franchisee must purchase products from the franchisor. A royalty as a percentage of sales does not allow such variation. Profits earned on sales will lead to efficient investment in development and promotion of new products to the benefit of both parties.

FRANCHISOR-FRANCHISEE RELATIONSHIPS: QUALITY CONTROL

Next to revenues, the most important element in the relationship between franchisees and franchisors is the monitoring of quality. The franchisee has an incentive to cheat on quality because he can then free ride on the quality provided by other franchises and acquire customers who expect higher quality than they will receive. Any given franchisee will lose only a share of the cost to the chain of this free riding, since some of the discouraged customers will cease patronizing the entire chain, and these losses will be shared by all members.

As a result, the franchisor must monitor quality of franchisees, and in establishing a franchise the franchisor should plan on such monitoring. There are two methods of monitoring quality. The franchisor can monitor inputs or outputs. Consider first inputs. There are three ways of monitoring inputs. The franchisor can require franchisees to buy directly from him; he can establish approved dealers and require buying from an approved dealer; or he can allow the franchisee to buy from anyone but require that any inputs meet technical specifications.

Requiring the franchisee to buy from the franchisor can have the additional advantage of enabling the franchisor to structure profits in relation to costs. It is also likely to be the cheapest way of assuring quality. Use of approved dealers may be cheaper if there are diseconomies of scale in production (so that costs would be higher if the franchisor made all of the inputs) or if, for example, freshness is an important quality input and franchisees are widely separated. Allowing the use of any product which meets technical specifications is likely to be quite expensive, since it will require extensive testing and monitoring. This method is unlikely to be worthwhile and probably has been used only in response to antitrust regulations.

In addition to monitoring inputs, franchisors also must monitor outputs. This monitoring is straightforward and consists of having anonymous buyers visit outlets and observe aspects of quality: freshness, cleanliness, service, etc. It is important to provide sufficient monitoring to eliminate free riding in order to continue selling franchises.

The ultimate sanction for quality violation is termination of the franchise. This will cost the franchisee a stream of quasirents (returns which would otherwise be earned on the investment in the franchise). The goal of the franchisor is to make sure that cheating on the franchise agreement does not pay. As the stream of quasirents (i.e., expected future profits for the franchisee) is larger, less monitoring is needed. As the stream is smaller, the potential loss is less of a deterrent and relatively more monitoring is needed. This would imply, for example, that as a franchise operation becomes more mature and the brand name becomes more valuable to franchisees, less monitoring will be needed because costs of shirking, in terms of lost future quasirents, will be greater. Newly established franchise systems will require extensive monitoring.

The payment of the franchise fee which will be forfeit if there is shirking is an example of a principle we have seen before, a bond, or a hostage. The franchisee puts forth a guarantee which is lost if he cheats on quality. During the period of the franchise, he earns a return on this investment, in the form of a quasirent. When the term is over, the franchisee still owns some rights, so he may receive back the value of the bond. This structure should be familiar by now.

Franchisors and franchisees will also need to cooperate on advertising in order to achieve the right amount. Franchisees will have an incentive to spend too little on advertising because the typical advertising message will tend to promote the franchise name as much as or more than the name and location of the particular franchisee. Therefore, most franchise contracts have provisions for the franchise either to advertise or to pay back the franchise for some or all of its advertising expenditure. The amount paid for by the franchisor should depend on the extent to which the advertising benefits the particular franchisee. For example, a single franchisee in a small town will gain much of the benefit from advertising in the local newspaper and should pay for some of this advertising. In a large city with many franchises, a dealer cooperative may be the efficient solution, since much of the benefit of the advertising will go to all sellers in proportion to their market shares. However, since some of the benefit will in all cases go to franchises outside the local advertising area, it is also efficient for the franchisor to pay for some advertising.

The franchisor will often provide other services for franchisees. These may include site selection, access to capital, and training. Since the franchisor has knowledge of the business, it is efficient for him to perform some of these services. Moreover, by providing training the franchisor can both insure standard practices in the chain and also increase the pool of potential franchisees; he need not search out franchisees with experience in the business. Provision of access to capital can also increase the pool of potential franchisees.

SUMMARY

If a firm decides to expand, it often can choose to use either owned outlets of franchised outlets. Some think that the choice rests on capital market considerations, but this is incorrect. The decision whether to use franchising or ownership is a complex one resting on issues of provision of incentives for efficient operation and control of quality. A common solution is to own outlets which are near the center of the operation (so that the owner can monitor their efficiency) or outlets which are in clusters (so that a paid employee can monitor their operations). This may entail beginning with franchises in distant locations and then buying them up as more stores are opened.

Since there are duties for both franchisees and franchisors in an ongoing relationship, it is important to draft contracts which give both parties incentives to perform their respective functions. Such contracts may have both franchise fees, royalties on sales, and profits earned on the sale of particular products from the franchisor to the franchisee. The main duty of a franchisee is to provide adequate quality. The main duty of a franchisor is to police franchisees' quality. Both share in such functions as advertising.

REFERENCES

Blair, Roger D., and Kaserman, David L. *Antitrust Economics,* Chapter 14. Homewood, Ill.: Richard D. Irwin, 1985.

Klein, Benjamin, and Saft, Lester F. "The Law and Economics of Franchise Tying Contracts." *The Journal of Law and Economics* 28 (1985):345.

Mathewson, G. Frank, and Winter, Ralph A. "The Economics of Franchise Contracts." *Journal of Law and Economics* 28 (1985):503.

Rubin, Paul H. "The Theory of the Firm and the Structure of the Franchise Contract." *The Journal of Law and Economics* 21 (1978):223. Reprinted in *Business Firms and the Common Law,* edited by Paul Rubin.

– 8 –

Creating a Reputation

Suppose you have a used 1985 Chevy to sell. You know that it is a "good" car, and good 85 Chevys are worth $2,000, but you would be willing to sell it for $1,700. Half of the 85 Chevys in existence are good cars, but the other half are "bad" cars, or lemons, and they are worth only $1,500. What will happen?

The answer is, given the facts, you will not be able to sell your car. You know that it is a good car and worth $2,000, so that someone buying it for $1,700, your selling price, would be getting a bargain. But a potential buyer does not know that it is a good car and, people being what they are, he will not automatically accept your statement that "Hey, this car is not a lemon." (Information in the market is asymmetric, in that one party, the seller, knows more than the other party, the buyer. Since you know the true value of the car, we say that you have *private information*.) Therefore, the buyer cannot know if the car is worth $2,000 or $1,500.

It might appear that he will be willing to pay $1,750 on the theory that this is the average value of both good and bad 85 Chevys. But this is not the way the market works. While the average value of all 1985 Chevys in existence is $1,750, the average value of all 1985 Chevys offered for sale will be much less. Let us examine the market process. If the price were to be $1,750, then those people who owned lemons (worth $1,500) would be glad to sell. On the other hand, most of those people who own good cars, worth $2,000, would not sell because they would only get $1,750. Therefore, if the price were initially $1,750, the value of cars actually offered for sale would be only $1,500, and soon the price would fall to this level. More importantly, only lemons would be traded. (The process of going from a market with all levels of quality traded to one with only lemons traded at low prices is an example of a market "unravelling," a concept introduced in Chapter 2.)

This point is quite general. In a market with asymmetric information and quality differences, it is quite possible for the equilibrium to be such that some worthwhile transactions (those which would in principle benefit both parties) cannot occur. This is called a *lemons market,* after the used car story which began the chapter. A lemons market is an example of what economists call a *market failure,* a general situation in which for some reason markets do not serve to allocate resources properly.

But where an economist sees a market failure, a businessman should see a chance for profit. After all, in this situation, there is a potential gain if only you can figure out how to capture it. The seller is willing to sell his car for $1,700 and it is worth $2,000, so if someone can come up with a way of convincing buyers that this car is not a lemon, he can make $300. Whether such a transaction can occur in this market depends on the exact assumption about the information structure. (Is it possible for some third party, a used car dealer or skilled mechanic to determine if a car is a lemon for less than $300?) However, in the general case of asymmetric information, sellers will attempt to devise mechanisms to overcome information problems.

METHODS OF GUARANTEEING QUALITY

As a seller or manufacturer, your first job is to decide just what level of quality you want to produce. In a market, there will be many levels of quality which can coexist. Some consumers pay more and want higher quality; other consumers prefer lower prices and are willing to accept lower quality. Profits have little to do with the level of quality; it is possible to have a very profitable firm which does not sell expensive, high-quality items. One important dimension of quality is variance. A McDonald's hamburger is by no means a gourmet meal, but the variance in quality is low; consumers know exactly what they are getting if they buy a McDonald's anywhere in the world. Thus, you must decide both the level of quality and the variance of quality which you want to offer. Once you have made this decision, then you must figure out a way to communicate your level of quality to consumers.

As a producer, you can determine the quality of your products. (That is, either you can decide what level of quality to produce or, at a minimum, you can find out what level of quality exists if you cannot control the level. We discuss below special problems which arise when there are costs to you of determining quality of products.) As above, products may be of high or low quality. Some consumers are willing to pay more for high quality, and they are willing to pay enough more to cover the cost of making high-quality products, so that the market should provide at least some of this quality products. This requires solving the lemons problem.

This problem is similar to others we have seen. The seller must be able to convince the buyer that it will not shirk or behave opportunistically. That is, the producer wants to be able to promise: "If you pay for high quality, I will sell only high-quality items." If he can convincingly make this statement, then the buyer will be willing to pay a higher price for the product, and both parties will be better off. The seller will make more profits, and the buyer will obtain the higher quality which she wants.

An explicit contract will not work in this market for several reasons. First, there are the common problems associated with writing complete contracts. These problems are exacerbated when the issue is some difficult-to-measure aspect of quality. We would have trouble suing McDonald's for breach of contract if it made its french fries too soggy, even if it had contracted not to do so, because the measurement of "too" soggy would be conceptually difficult. More importantly, the amounts at issue in many consumer contracts are so small that litigation would not be worthwhile.

Firms do offer warranties, which are contracts dealing with quality. However, the incentive for honoring a warranty is the cost to reputation of cheating, not the threat of litigation (except in cases of very expensive products, such as houses or cars). In general, we must rely on implicit, self-enforcing contracts.

The problem is then the familiar one of providing a hostage, or credible commitment. The seller wants to be able to offer items of a certain level of quality and charge a sufficiently high price to cover the additional costs of this quality. However, there is an incentive for the seller to cheat by charging for high quality but delivering low quality. In the short run, this will increase profits because low quality is less costly to produce. Since consumers are aware of this incentive, they will not be willing to pay for high quality unless the seller can credibly commit himself to offer it.

The hostage for performance must be in the familiar form of a quasirent stream. This stream may be a stream of profits, or a stream of returns on some investment. In either case, price of the product must be above marginal cost, and the difference must be high enough so that cheating by the firm does not pay. Thus, if you want to be a producer of high-quality products, you must be able to establish some stream of quasirents which will make cheating unprofitable. You must also have some way of communicating to consumers the information that cheating will not be profitable. This means that consumers must have some way of observing the investments associated with the quasirent stream.

There are several mechanisms available for producing this stream of returns. One option is to invest in *nonsalvageable,* firm-specific capital, where the use of this type of investment provides a credible commitment with respect to sales to other firms. Here, the investment must guarantee quality to consumers. For an investment to do this, it must be visible to consumers.

One obvious candidate is advertising. If a firms spends money advertising its own name, then this can be a signal to consumers that the firm will not cheat by degrading the name, for this behavior would reduce the value of the advertising to zero. Even advertising which seems non-informative (such as endorsements by celebrities) does in fact convey information; the information is that the firm has spent resources generating a quasirent stream and that it will lose the value of this investment if it behaves opportunistically with respect to its customers.

There are other, related investments which a firm can make to prove its trustworthiness. For example, investments in expensive signs, decor, and logos are useful because they become worthless if the firm cheats. Many law firms are elaborately (and expensively) furnished, and many banks use marble more extensively than might appear optimal. Again, both of these types of investments are examples of investment in nonsalvageable capital, and can serve to guarantee quality. Consumers know that if there is cheating, the value of these investments will be lost, and this acts as a bond for the firm.

A firm can also implicitly invest directly in a reputation. It can do this by offering high-quality items for sale at the price associated with low quality for some period of time. During this period, the firm loses money because quality is expensive and the firm is not charging for the level of quality it is producing. Some consumers will buy the product because they are paying for low quality, and so cannot lose even if the firm is lying about quality. Moreover, it would not pay for the firm to claim high quality unless it really was selling high quality, since the only return is repeat business and if consumers are deceived there will be no repeat business. Therefore, consumers will learn that the firm is indeed offering high quality. The investment might pay because the firm will later be able to recapture its investment by charging the higher price associated with high quality. This higher price is a return on the investment in generating a reputation, where the investment is in the form of losses associated with selling high quality at low-quality prices. Consumers are aware of the investment and therefore know that the firm will not cheat; if it does, it will lose the value of its past investment.

Note that, in general, there is a limit to the ability of a firm to use low price as a method of obtaining business in a market where quality is important and difficult to monitor. A high price can serve as a bond for the firm since a high price indicates that the firm has something to lose by offering low quality. Therefore, lowering price will eliminate this bond, and may lead consumers to believe that the firm is not offering quality. We saw this same selection mechanism in our discussion of the inability of some workers to offer to work for reduced wages and of the inability of borrowers to generate loans by offering higher interest rates.

Firms will seek those methods of investing in quality which are the lowest cost because this means that the quality guaranteeing price premium will be lower and thus sales will be greater. Thus, a firm should look for ways of generating a stream of quasirents at the lowest cost. Several principles are useful here.

One point is that sale of more kinds of items by the same firm lowers the cost of establishing a reputation. This is because cheating on quality in the sale of one item will cause consumers to devalue all items sold by the firm, and thus the firm will lose quasirents in many items. Owners of shopping malls can provide the same service if they monitor the quality of potential tenants and implicitly pledge the reputation of the entire mall as a bond for each tenant.

This has several implications. First, if you are an employee of a firm which has a reputation for producing quality, you can profitably extend this reputation to other high-quality items. On the other hand, if you sell a low-quality item, you will lose the stream of quasirents you are already earning on other, high-quality items. The implication is that you should constrain all your sales to lines which have about the same quality as your current lines. If you want to sell a lower quality line, a new brand name is desirable. If you want to improve the quality of your line, again a new line is desirable, and an investment in nonsalvageable capital, or in generating a reputation, would be useful.

A particular example of the power of many lines is shown by department stores and other stores which carry a large variety of products, and by malls. If such a retailer sells one low-quality item and disappoints consumers, then it will lose sales and quasirents not only from this item, but from all other lines it carries. Therefore, such stores will carefully monitor the quality of products they carry. This means that, if you are a manufacturer, it will pay you to invest substantial amounts to convince the highest quality outlet consistent with the quality of your product to carry your product because this is one of the most effective signals of quality available. If you want to open a retail store, then it pays to obtain a location at a mall which certifies quality. Again, recall that one variable is the level of quality you want to sell. In general, you should consider distribution through that level of retail establishment which specializes in the level of quality you want to offer for sale.

Department store reputations are often more valuable than reputations of some manufacturers. Therefore, many products are marketed under store names. Sears pioneered this marketing structure, but it is becoming more common.* If a manufacturer produces a house brand for a retailer, then at some point the manufacturer may develop a close relationship with the retail store. In this case, whether the manufacturing arm should be a subsidiary or an independent firm becomes a relevant issue. The considerations used in answering the make-or-buy decision should be used in making this determination.

In general, quality assurance is performed both by retail establishments and by manufacturers. In the last two chapters we discussed methods which can be used to create incentives for distributors to provide those elements of quality assurance which are most easily performed by distributors. In this chapter, we discuss those ways in which manufacturers themselves can best perform other aspects of quality assurance. The mix of efforts by each party will be a function of the costs to each of providing quality guarantees. For example, since the advent of television, manufacturers have been better able to communicate directly with consumers, and so the role of manufacturers in advertising and guaranteeing quality has increased. As a manager, you should be aware of the possibilities for quality guarantees from both retailers and producers, and structure incentives so both parties will create those aspects of quality best produced under their control.

An interesting issue is posed by prestige goods, such as expensive watches. Here, the value of the product to a consumer is created by its very price and exclusivity. If a manufacturer began to lower price and

* Reputation can work both ways. When the Consumer Product Safety Commission began recalling products, Sears found that whenever one of its products was recalled, it received a double mention in the press, since products were both made and sold by Sears. CPSC recall policies are such that having a product recalled does not indicate much about quality (or even safety) but nonetheless, this had substantial reputation costs for Sears.

increase sales, those consumers who had bought at the high price would lose and would (correctly) feel cheated. In other words, for these goods, the firm can behave opportunistically by reducing the price of the good. However, if the price is high, the firm will be earning a stream of quasirents on the good, and so it will pay to maintain the price. In advertising such a good, an important implicit message is that the firm will always maintain its quality level. One way of showing this is to prove that sales are sufficiently large so that the firm is currently earning a quasirent (but not so large as to lose the prestige value). Conspicuously spending large amounts on advertising for such goods will also be an important signal of quality.

ADVERTISING

We have discussed one function of advertising, the provision of a stream of quality assuring quasirents. However, advertising has many other functions. The purpose varies with the type of good involved, as does the ability of advertising to assure quality. Economists have identified three types of goods (or of characteristics of goods) with respect to advertising. These are *search* goods, *experience* goods, and *credence* goods. A search good is one whose quality can be detected before consumption, as in, "Is that shirt really white?" An experience good is one whose quality can be detected only after consumption, as in, "How does that pie taste?" A credence good is one whose quality cannot be detected even after consumption, as in, "Did I really need that tooth filled?" The way in which you should use advertising for your firm depends on which type of good you sell. (We also discuss advertising of negative characteristics of a product.)

Search Goods

For search goods, advertising serves a limited purpose. Consumers can themselves detect quality before purchase, so there is no need for advertising to carry any message about quality. (There is no "lemons problem" with this class of goods because information about quality is equally available to both parties to the transaction and lemons problems only arise if one party has more information than the other.) For these goods, advertising performs two functions. One is to provide information about price and availability. The second is to induce consumers to try the good. Advertising can then provide some indirect information about quality. In particular, it can inform consumers that if they examine the good, they will be likely to buy it. In advertising this class of goods, the ad should be informative, but there is little point in trying to be persuasive. Your goal is to tell the consumer where he can see the good, and perhaps rouse his desire to see the good, but once seen the good will speak for itself.

Experience Goods

Advertising as a quality signal is most important for experience goods. Of particular interest are those goods for which repeat purchases are important. Here, expensive advertising conveys the following message: "We have spent a lot on advertising this product. It would not be worth our while to spend this much if consumers were only going to buy the product once. Therefore, we think that it is a good enough product to generate repeat purchases, and it is in your interest to try it." Unless you want to convey this message, you should not spend money advertising a low-cost good whose profits depend on repeat sales.

The most difficult task for a seller is to sell a new experience good which is expensive enough to make a single purchase profitable for the seller. Advertising is of limited use here because consumers will be aware that it may pay the firm to deceive even if there will be no repeat business. For such a good, other mechanisms must be used. One is the possibility of creating a reputation by selling at a relatively low price until consumers learn the true quality associated with the good, as discussed above. Another option is convincing an appropriate retail store to carry the good. Finally, if a firm has some new good to sell and has no reputation, an arrangement with a firm which already has brand name recognition might be useful. In the limit, this arrangement might take the form of a merger. Nonetheless, it will be difficult to break into this type of market with a new brand.

Credence Goods

Credence goods are goods whose characteristics cannot be measured, even after consumption. The paradigm cases are repairs; a car or television, or human, will work well after a repair (e.g., replacement of a part or removal of an appendix) even if the repair was unneeded. There are strong incentives for sellers to offer unnecessary services in this case. How can a seller credibly commit not to do so?* There are various options, although none are perfect.

One option is establishing a reputation. This can be done by offering services at below cost for some period. During the period of reputation acquisition, the firm will suffer losses, but these can perhaps be recouped later.

In industries with credence characteristics, it is especially important to establish long-term relations with customers. If a firm expects a customer to return, then the firm would have something to gain from keeping the customer happy, and something (a stream of quasirents) to lose from cheating. Since customers know this, they understand that cheating would be costly for the firm. Therefore, in such industries, a viable strategy is to indicate to the customer that you expect repeat business. Mailing of cards reminding customers of scheduled maintenance, for example, would be useful. Establishing customer-specific records (as when a new physician spends time learning the medical history of a patient) would also be a method of establishing a stock of nontransferable capital. For such firms, advertising which stresses the length of business history and number of satisfied customers would also be useful.

Another option is to bundle service on the product with sale of the product itself. Thus, auto dealers can offer service departments. (This is less of an option with repair to humans.) This bundling implicitly makes the quasirents from sale of future automobiles a hostage for good service performance. Another option is a warranty. This requires the seller of the product to provide maintenance services. However, there are difficulties with warranties, as discussed below.

Negative Characteristics

In general, advertising naturally stresses positive characteristics of the good advertised. However, there are circumstances in which it may pay to advertise negative characteristics as well. This will be true if consumers are generally aware of the negative characteristic and if your product is less bad than others.

For an example, consider the current set of consumer preferences for avoidance of fats, and particularly of saturated fats, found in meat, milk, and in tropical oils. We are increasingly seeing advertisements

---

* Of course, one option is simply to cheat. However, following my standard practice of assuming but not encouraging opportunistic behavior, I will not discuss this option further.

claiming "No tropical oils." Many ads also stress the low level of fat in the product. Thus, even though fat is perceived as bad by consumers, it pays to advertise if your product has less of this bad than some others. Of course, the ad stresses the positive aspect (the low level) of the negative characteristic. If consumers knew nothing about the harm from fat, then you would not advertise the level. But once information about harmful effects becomes widespread, it will pay to advertise low levels. Of course, it may also pay to reformulate products with lower levels of harmful inputs so as to be able to advertise low levels.

This advertising is rational because sensible consumers will assume the worst; if your ad makes no mention of amount or type of fat, then a rational consumer will assume that your product has a lot of saturated fat. The process that generates information is like an unraveling process. Assume that initially only the firm with the lowest level of fat advertises. Then consumers will assume that all nonadvertising firms are at the bottom of the distribution. This will give the firm with the second lowest level an incentive to advertise; in the limit, all firms will advertise their exact level of fat except the very worst, and consumers will correctly believe that this firm is indeed the worst.

WARRANTIES (AND INSURANCE)

There would appear to be several benefits of warranties. First, consumers are risk averse and a warranty, like any form of insurance, reduces risk. When a consumer buys a warranty, he is paying the expected value of repairs. When a consumer does not buy a warranty, he accepts a lottery with the same expected value but with a chance of a very large payment. The warranty eliminates the risk of very large bills. Consumers are risk averse, and risk aversion means that the certain payment is preferred to the possibility of a large repair bill. Second, if the warranty is coupled with the sale of a product, the shirking with respect to sale of credence goods could be avoided since future sales of the product would serve as a hostage for repairs. Therefore, it is surprising that warranties are not more extensive and more complete. Indeed, in general there are many risks for which consumers do not buy insurance. This itself is a puzzle to be explained since risk aversion would lead one to expect more insurance against more adverse events than we actually observe. Understanding of the determinants of insurability will be useful in designing warranty contracts and many other contracts involving risk sharing.

Essentially, the limits to insurance are determined by two forms of opportunistic behavior which we have not yet explicitly identified, *adverse selection* and *moral hazard*. Adverse selection is presale opportunism, and moral hazard is postsale opportunism.

Adverse Selection

Consider the following problem: Assume that the average repairs on a car per year are $500. There are two types of drivers, with equal numbers of each. "Hard" drivers average $750 per year in repairs, and "easy" drivers average $250. Assume that consumers know what sort of driver they are. Now let us offer a warranty for auto repair. We know that the average is $500, so we charge this amount for our warranty (plus something for profit and administrative costs, but we may safely neglect this). Who will buy it? Clearly easy drivers will not buy the warranty (unless they are very risk averse) because the warranty costs twice as much as their expected costs. On the other hand, hard drivers will universally buy the warranty (unless they are very risk seeking) because it costs only half of their expected repair costs.

Of course, for you as a seller of warranties, this is not an equilibrium, because you have lost a lot of money. You have charged $500 for warranties, but your average cost will turn out to be $750. In the next period you will perforce charge $750 (unless you have gone bankrupt already). We can extend the story. Assume that the pool of hard drivers, with expected costs of $750, is itself made up of two groups. There are "really hard" drivers whose expected repair cost is $1,000 and "average hard" drivers whose expected cost is $500. Then when the price rises to $750, only the really hard drivers will buy the insurance, and again the company will lose money.

Obviously, we could go on, but the point should be clear. Adverse selection is a process of self-selection by consumers against insurance companies, and it places a limit on the sort of risks which are insurable. This is an unraveling process, much like the lemons story which began this chapter. Indeed, that story is one of adverse selection, where only low-quality cars are selected to enter the market. For adverse selection to be a problem, consumers must possess private information about themselves which is not available to the insurance company (or to the car buyer).

(An interesting example of adverse selection involves my home town, Washington, D.C. The city passed a law that made testing for AIDS or for HIV illegal in the sale of life insurance. All insurance companies immediately ceased selling insurance because they all realized that the law would lead to tremendous adverse selection. The law made the possession of information about HIV status private information because consumers could be tested and determine for themselves if they were infected, but the insurance companies could not obtain this information. Clearly, those who were infected would have found insurance a good buy. When testing is legal, the information is no longer private; it is available to parties on both sides of the transaction.)

Possibilities of adverse selection limit the sale of warranties. If consumers can determine their own risk class, then for any level of warranty, only the riskier class of consumers will buy the warranty. You can in part protect against this behavior by the design of your warranty. One option is to exclude classes of consumers who you know to be risky. Many warranties, for example, exclude commercial users. In general, excluding types of uses of the product which you know to be risky or to be associated with increased risk will be efficient. If you can design your product line so that some products appeal to riskier consumers, or to consumers who use the product more intensely, then you can offer different warranties for different products. For example, an automobile manufacturer might offer reduced warranty protection for sports cars, which tend to be driven more harshly than four-door sedans.

Moral Hazard

In order to reduce risks to their optimum level, it will often be efficient for both parties to a transaction to take precautions. For example, the manufacturer of an automobile should design the car so as to reduce need for maintenance, but it is also efficient for the buyer to take precautions, as by checking the oil and periodically changing it. Moral hazard is the shirking on this duty by the customer as a result of possession of insurance. If all auto repairs were fully warrantied, some drivers would not bother to check or change their oil because they would not bear the costs of this shirking. If a driver has theft insurance, he is less likely to lock his car.

In designing a warranty, then, it is important to reduce moral hazard. Again, particular terms in insurance policies or warranties can partially serve this function. For an automobile warranty to remain in effect, a proof of service might be required. (At one time, consumers were required to obtain service at the dealership to maintain the warranty, but such contracts have been inefficiently outlawed by a misapplication of the antitrust laws.)

Warranties should also exclude those aspects of the product whose condition is under control of consumers. For appliances, the finish will generally not be warrantied because the consumer can most cheaply preserve the finish. Small parts and parts which can break off will be excluded for similar reasons. A warranty covering the finish would lead consumers to inefficiently neglect the finish, and consumers can most easily avoid breaking off knobs and small plastic parts. Warranties covering these items would require manufacturers to charge a higher price for the warranty than its value to consumers. In designing warranties, you should look for those aspects of product quality controlled by consumers and try to devise ways of excluding them from warranty coverage.

On the other hand, for expensive parts which are not subject to abuse, a warranty would be desirable because the insurance provided would be valuable to consumers. Thus, many sealed parts (such as air conditioner compressors) are warrantied for extended periods of time. Consumers cannot affect the life of these parts, and so the warranty does not create moral hazard problems. If you can devise an extended warranty for such parts, you will have a valuable marketing tool.

An important class of damages which cannot generally be covered in a warranty are "consequential damages." These are damages over and above the cost of the product which are suffered if the product fails. An example would be spoilage of food in a failed refrigerator. Warranties commonly exclude consequential damages because their level can vary widely and because the manufacturer has no control over these damages.

It is important to note that risks can change as a result of insurance. If we measure the level of risk associated with some product and then offer a warranty, we may find that the actual observed risk is higher than the initial estimate because people will adapt to the insurance. It is for this reason that it is important to be sure only to warrant against risks which are not under the control of consumers.

"Secret Warranties"

Consider the following problem: You have made and sold a product. After many units have been sold, you learn that there is some major defect which affects 20 percent of the units. Any warranty associated with the product has already expired, so the defect will not be covered. The people who bought your product are obviously potential future customers, since they have already shown themselves to be willing to buy your product. However, those who buy the product and receive defective units will be dissatisfied and will not buy again, so you will lose 20 percent of your customers if you do nothing.

One option is to extend the warranty and advertise that "As of now, the Framistan on our Model 857 Widget is under an additional one-year warranty!" There are two disadvantages to this. First, and most important, you have now put forth a message to everyone that there is a defect in your product. Not only will the 20 percent of the consumers who have purchased the product learn of the defect; the other 80 percent of your customers who have not purchased such a defective unit, and everyone who has not bought at all from you (who sees the ad) will learn of the flaw. Second, you might be setting yourself up for a severe moral hazard problem. Anyone with a Model 857 might decide that it is worth getting a new Framistan, and therefore come in and claim one. (The ability to do this depends on the difficulty of simulating or creating a defect in a Framistan, a matter about which I have no direct knowledge.)

A solution is a "secret warranty." This is a policy whereby your dealers are told that if anyone complains about a defective Framistan in a Model 857, it is to be replaced free, but no one who does not complain is to be offered a replacement. This has the advantage of keeping many of the 20 percent of consumers who have received defective products happy without advertising to others that there is a problem with the product. Of course, some of the 20 percent will not complain and will just go elsewhere in the future, but in some circumstance the secret warranty is the best you can do.*

HIDING INFORMATION

In some circumstances, there are benefits from hiding information. When this situation arises, it will commonly be where there is some random variation in quality which is not under control of the product's producer and where it is costly to determine quality. The

---

* At various times, the Federal Trade Commission has misinterpreted the purpose behind such secret warranties and called them deceptive, but as of this writing that is no longer the FTC's policy. If they were outlawed, in general the result would be less repairs paid for by manufacturers, since the alternative would be to advertise the defect, and this would generally not pay.

advantage of hiding quality arises because it is sometimes possible to save on measurement costs through this policy.

For a homey example, consider potatoes. Some potatoes are OK and some are really good; a really good potato is worth $1.00 and an OK potato is worth $.50; it takes some time (say, five seconds per potato) to determine which are which. A grocery store buys a batch of 5,000 potatoes. The store samples 50 potatoes (spending 250 seconds) and determines that for this batch, half are OK and half are good. Therefore, this batch is worth $.75 per potato, or $3,750. How should the potatoes be sold? We can identify three options. (To simplify arithmetic, let each of these potatoes weigh one pound.)

First, the producer can sort the potatoes and offer the good ones for $1.00 and the OK ones for $.50. This will take about seven hours at five seconds per potato. If skilled potato sorters get $7.00 per hour, this will add $.01, about 1.5 percent, per pound to the price of potatoes. Second, the producer can put all the potatoes in a bin and let customers sort them themselves. For this to work, the producer will at first charge $1.00 per pound. Buyers will then sort through the potatoes until all of the good ones are gone. At this point, the producer will lower the price to $.50 per pound and sell the OK potatoes. (The store cannot simply offer the potatoes for $.75 because the good potatoes will go first, and then he will be left with 2,500 pounds of OK potatoes at $.75 per pound, and the OK potatoes will not sell for this price. An attempt to use this policy would generate a lemons market.) This search by consumers will also take seven hours of time (if potato buyers are as good at sorting as store clerks), but it will now be the time of customers, not of clerks. Nonetheless, time is time, and time is money, so that there is a real resource cost from the sorting.

Note that in both cases, there is no effect on the total value of the potatoes, but real resources have been wasted by the sorting. If a store can provide a way of saving this cost, it can benefit consumers and gain some business. The best option is to put all the potatoes in five-pound bags without sorting and sell each bag for $3.75, $.75 per pound. On average, each bag will contain half good and half OK potatoes, so consumers will get their money's worth. There is a real saving because no one, neither clerks nor consumers, has to sort each potato.

This mechanism only works for sellers with reputations. Otherwise, there is an incentive to cheat. That is, the store could pretend that it had not sorted the potatoes, but it could really sort them and sell only the bad ones for $.75, keeping the good ones to sell elsewhere for $1.00.

However, if a store does have a reputation, then this pricing method can save valuable resources, and generate business.

The example used so far has been potatoes, and indeed produce is often sold this way for exactly the reasons given. But it is not only mundane items such as potatoes and apples which are sold in packages to save on search costs. A more exciting good—uncut diamonds—is sold at wholesale in exactly the same way by De Beers, the major (almost only) diamond selling organization in the world. Ten times per year, a selected group of buyers is invited to 11 Harrowhouse, De Beers headquarters in London, and given the option to buy a package of diamonds at a take-it-or-leave-it price. (Buyers generally take it because if they refuse they are removed from the list, and the rights to buy are extremely valuable.) Again, the benefits of this scheme are in the saving on inspection costs. Other examples where this pricing mechanism has been used are in rental of movies to theaters and to TV stations. Whenever you are selling a good whose quality is somewhat random and not subject to absolute control, consider such a pricing mechanism.

SUMMARY

When quality is uncertain, markets may fail in that consumers who want and are willing to pay for high quality may nonetheless be unable to buy such quality. A market which fails in this way is called a "lemons market." In such markets, a firm that can manage to credibly convince consumers that it is selling high quality can make profits.

Several mechanisms are available to sellers to provide credible commitments that they will provide the level of quality which they promise. All such mechanisms require that price be above marginal cost, so that there is a quasirent associated with high quality. This quasirent acts as a bond, or hostage, and is lost if the firm cheats. Some mechanisms available for generating the quasirent stream are spending on advertising, and investment in nonsalvageable capital such as signs and expensive decor. An additional mechanism is investing in creating a reputation. A firm can do this by selling high-quality items at low-quality prices for some time, and then recapturing the investment by a price premium for high quality. Firms can guarantee quality by using already established brand names on new products. Certification by sellers such as department stores can also provide evidence of quality.

The functions of advertising vary with the type of good. For search goods, advertising primarily provides information about existence and availability. For experience goods, the quality assuring function of advertising is most important. It is particularly difficult to certify quality of credence goods. In some circumstances it pays to advertise negative characteristics of goods, because consumers will rationally believe that any nonadvertising firm makes the lowest level of quality.

Warranties are an additional method of certifying quality. However, because of two forms of opportunistic behavior, adverse selection (presale) and moral hazard (postsale), the possibilities of using warranties are limited. Firms can better design warranties if they understand these behaviors.

Finally, there are circumstances when it is in the interest of sellers to hide quality because this saves a real cost of sorting. This is sometimes true when selling goods whose quality is random and costly to determine.

REFERENCES

Ackerlof, George A. "The Market for Lemons: Qualitative Uncertainty and the Market Mechanism." *Quarterly Journal of Economics* 84 (1970):488.

Bresnahan, Timothy. "The Demand for Advertising by Medium: Implications for the Economies of Scale in Advertising." In *Consumer Protection Economics,* edited by Pauline M. Ippolito and David T. Scheffman. Washington D.C.: Federal Trade Commission, 1984.

Darby, Michael R., and Karni, Edi. "Free Competition and the Optimal Amount of Fraud." *Journal of Law and Economics* 26 (April 1973):67.

Grossman, Sanford. "The Informational Role of Warranties and Private Disclosure About Product Quality." *Journal of Law and Economics* 24 (1981):461.

Jordan, Ellen, and Rubin, Paul H. "An Economic Analysis of the Law of False Advertising." *Journal of Legal Studies* 8 (1979):116. Reprinted in *Business Firms and the Common Law,* edited by Paul Rubin.

Kenney, Roy W., and Klein, Benjamin. "The Economics of Block Booking." *Journal of Law and Economics* 26 (1983):497.

Klein, Benjamin, and Leffler, Keith B. "The Role of Market Forces in Assuring Contractual Performance." *Journal of Political Economy* 89 (1981):615.

Nelson, Philip. "Advertising as Information." *Journal of Political Economy* 81 (1974):729.

Nelson, Philip. "Information and Consumer Behavior." *Journal of Political Economy* 78 (1970):311.

Priest, George L. "A Theory of the Consumer Product Warranty." *The Yale Law Journal* 90 (1981):1297.

Shapiro, Carl. "Premiums for High Quality Products as Returns to Reputation." *Quarterly Journal of Economics* 98 (1983):615.

Stiglitz, Joseph E. "Imperfect Information in the Product Market." In *Handbook of Industrial Organization,* edited by Richard Schmalensee and Robert Willig. New York: North Holland, 1989.

Summary and Implications

The analysis and proposals in this book have been based on two basic principles. First, people are self-interested and opportunistic. Second, it is impossible to write complete contracts which take account of any and all possible events and which eliminate all forms of opportunism or cheating.*

Since people are opportunistic, they will attempt to engross for themselves as much as possible of the benefits of any arrangement or transaction. Since contracts are not and cannot be complete, we cannot use explicit, written, legally enforceable contracts to completely eliminate shirking or other forms of opportunism. As a result, other mechanisms must be used to minimize agency costs.

These two principles imply that there will be various forms of opportunism in transactions. The varieties of opportunism are limited. The same forms occur in all the types of markets we have examined, including input markets, labor markets, capital markets, and markets for final outputs, although various forms of opportunism are called different things in different markets, and the frequency of alternative forms of opportunism varies across markets.

One form of opportunism is precontractual opportunism, sometimes called adverse selection, a situation in which people select themselves in such a way as to penalize a trading partner. In this process, one party knows more than the other (knowledge is asymmetric, one party has private knowledge), and the knowledgeable party attempts to capitalize on this additional knowledge. In the limit, such opportunism can lead to a lemons market, and ultimately to the failure of a market to exist.

*A third principle is that people are risk averse. This principle is less important for the analysis than the other two, and is used only to eliminate contracts which put all of the risk on one party.

There may be extreme forms of precontractual opportunism. If a party enters into a contract with the explicit intention of capitalizing on the contract and engaging in some form of holdup after the contract is begun, then this may approximate fraud.

Other forms of opportunism are postcontractual. These forms arise in situations in which parties are already transacting. General names for these forms of opportunism include shirking, agency costs, and moral hazard.

One common form of postcontractual opportunism is quasirent expropriation, in which one party to a transaction attempts to engross for herself the returns associated with a fixed, or sunk, investment. This form of opportunism is often associated with holdup problems. Attempts to avoid such exploitation should govern the make-or-buy decision, or the level of vertical integration. Shirking is the term usually applied to opportunism in labor contracts. It entails efforts to further the goals of the employee, rather than the employer. Simple forms of shirking include unwarranted leisure on the job. More extreme forms entail distorted investment patterns for the firm, including misuse of free cash flow, associated with greatly reduced profitability for a firm, and also excessively conservative or excessively risky investment patterns.

To reduce the costs of opportunism in its assorted forms, various devices have been suggested. When possible, the most powerful device available for controlling these costs is the use of the market. Other possibilities include use of hostages and credible commitments to support exchange, so that parties who break their agreements will suffer losses. When such devices (which may take various forms, including for example joint ventures and reciprocal exchange) are available, they can reduce the costs of opportunism. Parties also engage in monitoring to control opportunism. Monitoring devices will include outside auditors and boards of directors.

Payment schemes can also be devised to reduce the costs of shirking. Most business transactions are governed by self-enforcing agreements, which, as the name suggests, are binding only because it pays for both parties to continue in the agreement. A two-part tariff (a fixed payment coupled with a variable payment) can align incentives and behavior, and so reduce shirking, although risk aversion limits the use of this method. Contests are methods of paying workers whereby relative performance is rewarded, and are useful if many workers face risks due to the same factors. Making decision makers the residual claimants is a powerful device to reduce shirking.

One of the most important tools available for controlling opportunism is creation of a reputation. A reputation for non-opportunistic behavior (for a person and, more importantly, for a firm) is an efficient method of guaranteeing that cheating will not occur, and therefore an efficient method of supporting exchange. On the other hand, it is important in vertical transactions to devise methods of eliminating incentives of one party to free ride on the reputation of other parties. Franchise contracts, for example, are aimed at reducing this sort of free riding.

In general, it is in the interests of all parties to an exchange to reduce opportunism to the lowest possible levels. Since parties to transactions are rational, they will anticipate some shirking and will adjust their payments accordingly. Therefore, the more a party can commit herself not to shirk, the higher the payment she can receive from her trading partner. Thus, you should look for ways to limit opportunism in all contracts to which you are a party, and you should explain to your trading partners ways in which suggested arrangements can work to reduce shirking.

In the special case of the behavior of management with respect to stockholders, an additional control is the law of fiduciary duties. A manager in charge of a company has particular legal obligations, in addition to those which apply to parties to arms-length contracts. These responsibilities include: duties to disclose, over and above the corresponding obligation imposed on traders under normal contracts; more open-ended duties to act in the interests of shareholders, in addition to any specific duties specified in the agreement; and greater-than-normal restrictions on rights to receive benefits associated with the position. These restrictions may be explained because of the greater-than-average power of peak managers, and the difficulty stockholders have in policing these managers. In addition, courts are more likely to use language regarding morals and other forms of normative rhetoric in finding liability for violating any of these obligations. We now turn to the role of morality in policing contracts in general.

ETHICS

To the extent that opportunism may be viewed as a form of cheating, it might appear that we could rely on ethical behavior as a way to control shirking. Nonetheless, in writing this book I have downplayed the role of ethics. There are several reasons for this decision. (As an economist, I may not have any particular ability to even define ethics. I will use the term as being synonymous with efficient. Any behavior which is efficient will be considered ethical. Efficient behavior is value maximizing.)

First, it does not pay for you to be more ethical than those which whom you are transacting. If all parties to transactions routinely engage in opportunism and you do not, then you will find yourself being taken advantage of and will ultimately be eliminated from the market.

Second, it will not always be possible to determine the meaning of ethical behavior. I believe that (perhaps for evolutionary reasons) humans have the ability to convince themselves that actions which are in their own interest are also moral. An outside observer (if properly trained) can sometimes determine what is truly ethical, but not always; a party to an agreement would have much more difficulty. A rule of behavior which said "Always act ethically" would not give much useful guidance. Indeed, much behavior which appears ethical to many is nonetheless inefficient (in an economic sense) and therefore leads to reduced wealth in society. (For one example, many feel that it is morally right to help farmers. The effect of policies aimed at this goal is often to increase costs of food, and the poor spend a disproportionate share of their incomes on food. Therefore, the effect of many apparently ethical policies is increased hunger.)

Third, and perhaps most important, there is little reason to rely on ethics for the types of situations discussed in this book. This book deals only with situations in which parties are already transacting with each other. In such circumstances, it is possible to devise side payments so that it will pay for parties to engage in all efficient transactions (or, in my terms, to behave ethically). Therefore, in the types of situations covered in this book it is possible to construct efficient side payments. For example, a golden parachute is a side payment to a manager to induce the manager to sell the firm when this is efficient and in the interests of stockholders. In general, the transactions discussed here would create joint gains, and side payments can be used to ensure that the gains are indeed realized.

In one sense, then, the purpose of the various transactions discussed in this book is to eliminate the need for relying on ethics to achieve efficiency. What I have attempted to do is to indicate ways in which we can structure transactions to make it in the interests of all parties to the deal to behave ethically and efficiently. Because there is a limit to our willingness to reduce our own incomes in order to benefit others (another possible meaning of ethics), there are advantages of structuring transactions in ways which lead us to provide such benefits without harming ourselves. To an economist, this is a real benefit of efficient transactions.

REFERENCES

Clark, Robert C. "Agency Costs Versus Fiduciary Duties." In *Principals and Agents,* edited by John W. Pratt and Richard J. Zeckhauser. Boston: Harvard Business School Press, 1985.

Posner, Richard A. *The Economics of Justice,* Part 1. Boston: Harvard University Press, 1981.

Rubin, Paul H. "Evolved Ethics and Efficient Ethics." *Journal of Economic Behavior and Organization* 3 (1982):161.

Glossary

Active investor An investor who takes an active role in monitoring the performance of a company, a role commonly performed by the financial firm which organizes a leveraged buyout (LBO).

Adverse selection A form of opportunism associated with self-selection in certain insurance markets. Adverse selection can lead to a lemons market.

Agency costs Costs of the divergence in goals between hiring party and hired party (i.e., between the principal and the agent). These may be divided into monitoring expenditures by the principal, bonding expenditures by the agent, and a residual loss.

Agent An actor who is hired by another, called the principal.

Asymmetric information A situation where one party to a transaction possesses more information than the other party. Such information can sometimes lead to exploitation, and sometimes to a lemons market.

Bond A commitment by a worker to a firm, analogous to a "hostage," often used to reduce agency costs.

Closely held corporation A corporation with a limited number of shareholders whose stock is not publicly traded. This method of finance is intermediate between debt and equity.

Contest A method of paying workers in which payment depends on relative performance of all workers.

Corporate control transaction A transaction which leads to a change in the ownership or control of a corporation, including leveraged buyouts (LBOs) and takeovers, both friendly and hostile.

Credence good A good whose quality cannot always be detected even after consumption, as in a repair. (Did the car really need a new carburetor?) Contrasted with experience goods and search goods.

Credible commitment An agreement which can be enforced and can therefore be relied on.

Deadweight loss A loss to one party which is not compensated for by a gain to anyone else; the essence of inefficiency. Monopolies cause deadweight losses, and so do contracts which allow excessive shirking.

Economies of scale Cost savings from producing more units of some product.

Economies of scope Cost savings from producing additional types of products in the same facility.

Event study A technique for determining the effect of some event on the stock price of a firm; used for measuring the effects of various antitakeover methods. It is proposed that management make use of this technique to evaluate various policies before undertaking them.

Experience good A good whose quality can be detected only after purchase; contrasted with credence goods and search goods.

Exploitable quasirent A return on "sunk" investments. A firm may make an investment with the expectation of earning some return, but once an investment is sunk, the firm will often continue to operate it even if it is not earning as much as it expected, as long as it is earning more than the best alternative. The difference is the exploitable (or appropriable) quasirent.

Externality A cost created by one party but borne by another, as when a restaurant in a franchise chain degrades quality and lowers the reputation of the chain.

Free cash flow Cash flow earned by a firm in excess of that required to fund all projects with positive net present values when discounted at the relevant cost of capital; excess free cash flow is viewed as a reason for many takeovers.

Free riding Earning profits on the efforts of others, as when a low-quality franchise outlet earns profits because it is perceived as being like other, high-quality outlets.

Fundamental transformation The shift from a competitive situation before some specific investment is undertaken to a bilateral monopoly after the investment.

General human capital Human capital which is valuable in many firms, as opposed to specific human capital.

Going private A transaction in which a public corporation becomes privately held and in which equity is replaced by debt. The purpose is to transfer free cash flow to investors. The most common form is the leveraged buyout (LBO).

Golden parachute Payment to management of a target firm if an acquisition is successful. This can serve to motivate managers, and also to compensate them for non-contractual implicit agreements.

Greenmail Targeted stock repurchases; repurchase of stock held by a potential acquirer of a firm. It is possible for this to be in stockholders' interests, but the evidence is mixed.

Holdup A situation in which someone is in a position to exploit some vulnerability of a firm. Such exploitation is often an example of opportunistic behavior. The amount which can be exploited is the exploitable quasirent.

Hostage A valuable asset which will be forfeit if a contract is not honored; a method of creating a credible commitment.

Implicit contract An unwritten agreement with particular payment schedules and incentives. Since the agreement is unwritten (because complete specification would be impossible), there are no legal penalties and the contract must be self-enforcing.

Last-period problem If there is a last period specified in some contracts, they will unravel and therefore are not self-enforcing.

Lemons market A market failure caused by asymmetric information about quality, with only low quality goods sold.

Leveraged buyout (LBO) A transaction in which a group of investors, commonly including a management team, buys a public company and takes it private, replacing equity with debt.

Leveraged recapitalization (recap) A scheme by which managers pay a large dividend to stockholders, where the dividend is approximately equal to the total value of each share. An alternative to an LBO.

Liquidated damages A damage payment specified in a contract which is judged equal to actual losses.

Market failure A situation in which some factor keeps a market from functioning, so that some worthwhile transactions do not occur. An example is a lemons market.

Monitoring Efforts to make sure that another party to an agreement (e.g., an agent) obeys his contract and does not behave opportunistically.

Moral hazard A form of opportunism associated with a failure to take efficient precautions because of the presence of insurance.

Nonsalvageable capital An investment which becomes worthless if the investor breaches some agreement; a method of establishing a credible commitment.

Opportunistic behavior A situation in which some actor takes advantage of a position which has arisen as a result of an exchange of some sort. An important goal of management is to avoid being put in a position of becoming the victim of opportunistic behavior. Sometimes defined as "self-interest seeking with guile."

Plastic Resources are said to be more plastic as they are more flexible and can be used for more activities. There is a greater chance for opportunism as resources are more plastic.

Poison pill Provisions in corporate charters for issuing of additional stock in the event of a hostile tender offer, of for other provisions making takeovers expensive and difficult. Generally not in the interests of shareholders.

Principal An actor who hires another, called the agent.

Private information Information possessed by only one party to a transaction, which can lead to adverse selection.

Punitive damages A damage payment specified in a contract which is held to be greater than actual damages; not generally enforceable.

Quasirent A return on fixed investment. Once a fixed investment is made, its return can be exploited. A quasirent can also serve as a bond or hostage to guarantee performance.

Redeployable Capital which is redeployable can be easily shifted from one use to another.

Residual claimant That actor who has claims on any profits or losses for the enterprise.

Residual decision right Right to control decisions within a firm; an important issue when circumstances may change.

Residual rights Those rights associated with the use of some asset which are not specified in the contract dealing with the use of the asset, as opposed to specific rights. The party with residual rights is the owner of the asset.

Risk aversion A dislike of bearing financial risk. Since most people are risk averse, workers and investors must be paid additional amounts for bearing risk.

Search good A good whose quality can be detected before purchase; contrasted with credence goods and experience goods.

Self-enforcing agreement An agreement which provides incentives so that no outside enforcement is needed.

Self-selection At times, a decision by a party to accept or not to accept an offered contract is a method of determining the intentions of the party; in this case, we say that the party has self-selected based on his acceptance or rejection of the offer.

Shark repellent various forms of supermajority voting requirements, aimed at reducing risks of takeovers. Some of these are efficient (in the interests of stockholders) and some are not.

Shirking For a worker, the equivalent of opportunistic behavior, or not providing everything contracted for to an employer.

Specific asset An asset which is required for some activity. The existence of specific assets often leads to possibilities of opportunistic behavior.

Specific human capital Human capital which is valuable only in a particular firm, as opposed to general human capital.

Specific performance A court order to fulfill the exact terms of a contract. This is generally not available, as the courts usually award only damages.

Specific rights Those rights associated with the use of some asset which are specified in the contrast dealing with the use of the asset, as opposed to residual rights. The party with residual rights is the owner of the asset.

Sunk investment An investment which is already done and which cannot in the short run be undone. The returns on sunk investment are exploitable quasirents.

Team A group of workers who jointly produce some output in situations where the contribution of each is difficult or impossible to measure; the output of the team is greater than the summed outputs of the individuals.

Two-part tariff A payment schedule consisting of a fixed payment and a variable payment. This type of contract can be used both to provide incentives and to reduce risk.

Unravelling A contracting process which is not stable because it pays to breach in the last period, and each period successively becomes the last period.

Vertical integration Common ownership of more than one stage of production, justified to avoid being held up.

Bibliography

Ackerlof, George A. "The Market for Lemons: Qualitative Uncertainty and the Market Mechanism." *Quarterly Journal of Economics* 84 (1970):488.

Alchian, Armen, and Demsetz, Harold. "Production, Information Costs, and Economic Organization." *American Economic Review* 62 (1972):777. Reprinted in *The Economic Nature of the Firm,* edited by Louis Putterman.

Becker, Gary S., and Stigler, George J. "Law Enforcement, Malfeasance, and Compensation of Enforcers." *Journal of Legal Studies,* 3 (1974):1.

Coase, Ronald. "The Nature of the Firm." *Economica* 4 (1937): 386. Reprinted in *The Economic Nature of the Firm,* edited by Louis Putterman.

Jensen, Michael C. "Agency Costs of Free Cash Flow, Corporate Finance, and Takeovers." *American Economic Review* 76 (1986):323.

Jensen, Michael C., and Meckling, William H. "Theory of the Firm: Managerial Behavior, Agency Costs and Ownership Structure." *Journal of Financial Economics.* 3 (1976):306. Reprinted in *The Economic Nature of the Firm,* edited by Louis Putterman.

Klein, Benjamin; Crawford, Robert; and Alchian, Armen. "Vertical Integration, Appropriate Rents, and the Competitive Contracting Process." *Journal of Law and Economics* 21 (1978):297. Reprinted in *The Economic Nature of the Firm,* edited by Louis Putterman.

Klein, Benjamin, and Leffler, Keith B. "The Role of Market Forces in Assuring Contractual Performance." *Journal of Political Economy* 89 (1981):615.

Macaulay, Stewart. "Non-Contractual Relations in Business." *American Sociological Review* 28 (1963):55.

Manne, Henry. "Mergers and the Market for Corporate Control." *Journal of Political Economy* (1965):110. Reprinted in *The Economic Nature of the Firm,* edited by Louis Putterman.

Pratt, John W., and Zeckhauser, Richard J., eds. *Principals and Agents: The Structure of Business.* Boston: Harvard Business School Press, 1985.

Putterman, Louis, ed. *The Economic Nature of the Firm: A Reader.* New York: Cambridge University Press, 1986.

Rubin, Paul H. *Business Firms and the Common Law: The Evolution of Efficient Rules.* New York: Praeger, 1983.

Schmalensee, Richard, and Willig, Robert, eds. *Handbook of Industrial Organization.* New York: North Holland, 1989.

Telser, Lester G. "Why Should Manufacturers Want Fair Trade?" *Journal of Law and Economics.* 3 (1960):86.

Williamson, Oliver E. *The Economic Institutions of Capitalism*. New York: Free Press, 1985. (Oliver Williamson has written many other books and articles which have been influential in developing transactions cost economics. I cite his recent book because this is the most useful for my purposes, but his influence is much older than this indicates.)

Index

Ackerlof, George A., 161, 173
Acquisitions of businesses, 18–21
Active investors, 76
Adverse selection, 155–156,
   162–163
Advertising
   cooperative, 130, 142–143
   of credence goods, 151–153
   of experience goods, 151, 152
   of negative characteristics,
      153–154
   quasirent stream generation with,
      148
   of search goods, 151–152
Agency costs, 48, 163
Agency theory, 47–50
Agents, outside, 65–67
Alchian, Armen A., 22, 68, 93, 173
Antitrust laws, 11, 139n
Arrow, Kenneth J., 68
Asset ownership, 16–17, 28
Asset specificity, 8–13, 28
Asymmetric information, 13, 145,
   146
Attorneys, outside, 65–67
Auditors, outside, 82

Bankruptcy, 75–76
Baysinger, Barry D., 110
Becker, Gary S., 68, 173
Bilateral exchange, 34–36
Blair, Roger D., 22, 132, 143

Board of directors, 82
Bonding, 58–62
Bresnahan, Timothy, 161
Brickley, James A., 111
Business acquisitions and sales,
   18–21
Butler, Henry D., 110

Capital
   firm-specific, 89
   franchising and, 134–136
   human, 55–57, 87
   nonsalvageable, 33, 148
   raising, see Finance
   vertical integration and, 15–16
Clark, Robert C., 166
Clarkson, Kenneth W., 41
Closely held corporations, 83–87
Coase, Ronald, 22, 173
Coffee, John C., Jr., 93
Collateral, 77
Consequential damages, 157
Contests, 62–64, 126
Contingent contracts, 66–67
Contract law, 11
Contracts
   acquisitions and sales of busi-
      nesses and, 18–21
   efficient, 24–25
   employment agreements, see Em-
      ployment agreements
   enforced by courts of law, 25–28

Contracts (*continued*)
  golden parachutes, 106–107
  hostages and, 31–32
  implicit, 118, 124
  intrafirm, 38–39
  lawyer partnerships and, 88–89
  opportunistic behavior and, 7–8,
    24–27, 162–163
  requirements, 128–129
  self-enforcing, 29–31, 124–131
  warranties, 147, 154–158
Cooperative advertising, 130,
  142–143
Courts of law, contracts enforced
  by, 25–28
Covenant not to compete, 56–57
Crawford, Robert, 22, 173
Credence goods, 151–153

Damages, 27–28, 157
Darby, Michael R., 161
Deadweight losses, 96
Debt financing, 75–79
  conversion of equity financing to,
    96–100
  shirking avoidance with, 102
Demsetz, Harold, 68, 93, 173
Department store reputations,
  149–150
Distribution, 117–132
  dealer-provided services desired
    by manufacturers, 120–124
  exclusive dealing, 128–129
  exclusive territories, 127–128
  franchising, *see* Franchising
  incentives for retailers, 124–126
  maximum purchase require-
    ments, 129–130
  minimum price restrictions, 126
  producer provision of services,
    130
  reasons for manufacturer restric-
    tions, 118–120
  tying, 130–131

Easterbrook, Frank H., 93
Eatwell, John, 41, 46
Eccles, Robert G., 41
Economies of scale, 23, 67
Economies of scope, 23
Elimination career ladders, 63
Employee Stock Ownership Plans
  (ESOPS), 89–90
Employment agreements, 47–68
  agency theory, 47–50
  bonding, 58–62
  contests, 62–64
  outside agents, 65–67
  risk aversion and, 51–55
  specialized skills and training
    and, 55–57
  team production and, 57–58
  wage structure within hierarchies,
    64–65
Epstein, Richard A., 69
Equity financing, 79–82
  conversion to debt financing,
    96–100
Ethics, 164–166
Event studies, 95, 112–113
Exclusive dealing, 129
Exclusive territories, 127–128
Experience goods, 151, 152
Exploitable quasirents, *see* Quasirents

Fair price amendment, 108
Faith, Roger L., 93
Fama, Eugene F., 93
Finance, 73–93
  closely held corporations, 83–87
  debt, *see* Debt financing
  equity, *see* Equity financing
  hybrid, 83
  organizational structure and,
    87–91
  separation of ownership and con-
    trol and, 74
  See also Takeovers

Firm-specific capital, 89
Fischel, Daniel R., 93
Franchising, 134–143
 characteristics of, 134
 vs. ownership, 134–138
 quality control and, 141–143
 revenues and, 139–141
Free cash flow, 81, 98–101, 103–104
Free riding, 119–131
 example of, 119
 exclusive dealing and, 129
 exclusive territories and, 128
 freshness maintenance and,
  121–122
 incentives to reduce, 124–126
 in-store service and, 122
 inventories and, 123
 maximum purchase requirements
  and, 129–130
 minimum price restrictions and,
  126–127
 producer provision of services
  and, 130
 product demonstration and,
  120–121
 promotional efforts for marginal
  consumers and, 122
 quality certification and, 121
 tying and, 130–131
 undesirable dealer behavior and,
  124
Freshness, maintenance of, 121–122
Friendly takeovers, 94
Fundamental transformation, 10–11

General human capital, 55–57
Geographic asset specificity, 12
Gilson, Ronald J., 22, 93
Going private, 94, 96–102
Goldberg, Victor, 22
Golden parachutes, 106–107
Greenmail, 107–108
Grossman, Sanford J., 22, 161

Hart, Oliver D., 22, 41
Heimer, Carol A., 41
Hiding information, 158–160
Hierarchial structure of internal
 exchange, 39–40
Hierarchies, wage structure within,
 64–65
Higgins, Richard S., 93
Holdup problems, 4–8
 asset specificity and, 8–10
 contractual difficulties in avoid-
  ance of, 7–8
 example of, 5–6
 mobile-specific assets and, 28
 vs. monopoly position, 10–11
 source of supply and, 15
Holmstrom, Bengt R., 22, 69
Hostages, 31–32
Hostile takeovers, 94, 99
Human capital, 55–57, 87
Hybrid financing, 83

Implicit contracts, 118, 124
Indemnification, 21
Influence activities, 49
Information
 asymmetric, 13, 145, 146
 hiding, 158–160
 issues in sales of businesses,
  20–21
 private, 145
 verification of, 20–21
 vertical integration and problems
  of, 13
Inputs, *see* Employment agree-
 ments; Make-or-buy decision
Insurance, 154–158
Integration, vertical, 4, 8–10
Interdivisional transfers, 43–45
Internal labor markets, 58
Intrafirm transactions, 38–40, 43–45
Inventories, 123
Ippolito, Pauline M., 161
Ippolito, Richard, 69

Jarrell, Gregg A., 111
Jensen, Michael C., 93, 111, 173
Joint ventures, 35, 45
Jordan, Ellen, 161
"Junk" bonds, 78–79, 84–85, 98–99

Karni, Edi, 161
Kaserman, David L., 22, 132, 143
Katz, Michael I., 133
Kenney, Roy W., 161
Kieschnick, Robert L., Jr., 111
Klein, Benjamin, 22, 93, 133, 143,
    161, 173
Klein, William A., 93
Knoeber, Charles R., 41, 111

Labor contracts, see Employment
    agreements
Last-period problem, 30
Law firms, 87–89
Lazear, Edward P., 69
Leasing, 78
Leffler, Keith B., 161, 173
Lehn, Kenneth, 93, 111
Lemons market, 146
Leveraged buyouts (LBOs), 94,
    96–101
Leveraged recapitalization, 100
Licensing, mandatory, 33
Liquidated damages, 27
Litigation, 27, 95, 105
Loan collateral, 77
Long-term vs. short-term invest-
    ment, 102–103

Macaulay, Stewart, 41, 173
Macey, Jonathan R., 111
Make-or-buy decision, 3–22
    managerial basis of, 3–4
    presumption of market provision
        of inputs, 4
    See also Market provision of in-
        puts; Vertical integration
Management market, 91

Mandatory licensing, 33
Manne, Henry, 111, 173
Manufacturers, 117–132
    dealer-provided services desired
        by, 120–124
    direct provision of services by,
        130
    exclusive dealing restriction of,
        128–129
    exclusive territories restriction of,
        127–128
    incentives for retailers provided
        by, 124–126
    maximum purchase restriction of,
        129–130
    minimum price restriction of, 126
    product quality and, see Reputa-
        tion
    reasons for restrictions on re-
        tailers, 118–120
    tying restriction of, 130–131
Market failure, 146
Marketing, see Distribution; Fran-
    chising; Reputation
Market provision of inputs, 23–45
    bilateral exchange and, 34–36
    conditions leading to opportunis-
        tic behavior, 5–6
    contracts enforced by courts of
        law and, 25–28
    contractual difficulties in avoid-
        ance of opportunistic behavior,
        7–8
    efficient contracts and, 24–25
    hostages and, 31–32
    mandatory licensing and, 33
    mobile specific assets and, 28
    monitoring and, 36–38
    presumption of, in make-or-buy
        decision analysis, 4
    price constraints and, 34
    reputation and, 35–36
    self-enforcing agreements and,
        29–31
    sunk investments and, 32–33

Market simulation, 38–39
Marvel, Howard P., 133
Mathewson, G. Frank, 133, 144
Maximum purchase restriction, 129–130
McChesney, Fred S., 111
Meckling, William H., 93, 111, 173
Mergers, *see* Takeovers
Milgate, Murray, 41, 46
Milgrom, Paul R., 69
Miller, Roger L., 41
Minimum price restrictions, 126–127
Mitchell, Mark, 111
Mnookin, Robert H., 93
Mobile-specific assets, 28
Monitoring, 36–38
  debt financing and, 76–77
  distribution and, 125
  equity financing and, 82
  franchising and, 137, 138, 141–143
Monopoly, 10–11
Monteverde, Kirk, 41
Moral hazard, 156–157
Mork, Randall, 93, 111
"Most favored nation" pricing clause, 34
Muris, Timothy J., 41
Murphy, Kevin M., 133
Myerson, Roger B., 46

Negative characteristics, advertising of, 153–154
Nelson, Philip, 161
Netter, Jeffrey M., 111
Newman, Peter, 41, 46
Nonsalvageable capital, 33, 148

On-the-job consumption, 79–80
Opportunistic behavior, 4–8
  adverse selection, 155–156, 162–163
  agency costs, 48, 163
  by attorneys, 67

bonding and, 58–62
characteristics of, 4–5
conditions leading to, 5–6
debt financing and, 76
holdup problems, *see* Holdup problems
postcontractual, 163
product quality and, 147–151
quasirents, *see* Quasirents
shirking, *see* Shirking
Opportunistic behavior control, 163–164
  asset specificity and, 8–13, 28
  bilateral exchange, 34–36
  closely held corporations, 84
  contracts and, 7–8, 24–28, 162–163
  ethics and, 164–166
  hostages, 31–32
  intrafirm transactions and, 38–40, 43–45
  mandatory licensing, 33
  monitoring, 36–38
  price constraints, 34
  reputation and, *see* Reputation
  self-enforcing agreements, 29–31
  sunk investments, 32–33
Organizational structure, finance and, 87–91
Outside agents, 65–67
Outside auditors, 82

Pashigian, B. Peter, 93
Physical asset specificity, 12–13
Piecework contracts, 49–51
Plastic industries, 76
Poison pills, 108–109
Posner, Richard A., 166
Pratt, John W., 41, 68, 69, 166, 173
Precontractual opportunism, *see* Adverse selection
Price constraints, 34
Price restrictions, minimum, 126–127
Pricing restrictions, 117

Priest, George L., 161
Private information, 145
Product demonstration, 120–122
Product quality, *see* Reputation
Promotional efforts for marginal
    consumers, 122
Proxy contests, 94
Punitive damages, 27
Putterman, Louis, 22, 111, 173

Quality certification, 121
Quality control, in franchising,
    141–143
Quasirents
    franchising and, 142
    as hostages, 32
    make-or-buy decision and, 5, 6,
        9–11, 13–15
    product quality and, 147–149
    retailers and, 125–130
Quotas, 128

Radner, Roy, 46
Recapitalization, leveraged, 100
Reorganizations, *see* Takeovers
Reputation, 145–161
    advertising and, *see* Advertising
    bonding and, 61
    distribution and, 123
    hiding information, 158–160
    market provision of inputs and,
        35–36
    methods of guaranteeing quality,
        146–151
    warranties and, 147, 154–158
Requirements contract, 128–129
Resale price maintenance, 126–127
Residual claimants, 73, 74, 78,
    87–88
Residual decision right, 12
Residual rights, 16
Retailers
    exclusive dealing restriction on,
        128–129

exclusive territories restriction
    on, 127–128
incentives for, 124–126
maximum purchase restriction
    on, 129–130
minimum price restrictions on,
    126
reasons for manufacturer restric-
    tions on, 118–120
services desired by manufacturers
    of, 120–124
tying restriction on, 130–131
Revenues, franchising, 139–141
Risk aversion, 51–55, 154
Rosen, Sherwin, 69
Rubin, Paul H., 41, 69, 144, 161,
    166, 173

Saft, Lester F., 143
Sales of businesses, 18–21
Scale, economies of, 23
Scheffman, David T., 161
Schmalensee, Richard, 22, 42, 69,
    133, 161, 173
Schwert, G. William, 111
Scope, economies of, 23
Search goods, 151–152
Secret warranties, 157–158
Segal, Harvey H., 111
Self-enforcing agreements, 29–31,
    124–131
Self-selection, 25, 155
Separation of ownership and con-
    trol, 74
Shapiro, Carl, 161
Shark repellants, 108
Shavell, Steven, 41
Shedd, Peter, 69
Shelf space, charging for, 126
Shirking, 48–52, 163
    by attorneys, 67
    bonding and, 58–62
    closely held corporations and,
        84–87
    contract labor and, 49–51

equity financing and, 79–80, 82
finance and, 75
forms of, 48–49
franchising and, 137, 140,
    141–142
free riding, *see* Free riding
leveraged buyouts and, 100
management market and, 91
moral hazard, 156–157
by retailers, *see* Free riding
risky contracts and, 52, 53
takeovers and, 95, 100–103
team production and, 58
Shleifer, Andrei, 93, 111
Short-term vs. long-term invest-
    ment, 102–103
Single proprietorships, 91
Site-created asset specificity, 12
Skills, specialized, 55–57
Specialized skills and training,
    55–57
Specific assets, 8–13, 28
Specific human capital, 55, 56
Specific performance, 27–28
State law, takeovers and, 109
Stigler, George J., 68, 173
Stiglitz, Joseph E., 69, 161
Sunk investments and, 32–33
Supply, secure source of, 15

Takeovers, 94–110
    avoidance of, 100–103
    decision to implement, 103–104
    event studies and, 95, 112–113
    general characteristics of, 94–95
    going private, 94, 96–102
    litigation and, 95, 105
    provisions hindering, 104–109
    shirking and, 95, 100–103
Targeted block stock repurchases,
    107–108
Team production, 57–58
Technological explanation for verti-
    cal integration, 14–15

Teece, David J., 41
Telser, Lester G., 42, 133, 173
Tender offers, 94
Term of contract, 27
Territories, exclusive, 127–128
Third-party certification, 21
Time-related issues in sales of busi-
    nesses, 19–20
Tirole, Jean, 22, 69
Tollison, Robert D., 93
Training, specialized, 55–57
Two-part tariffs, 54–55, 66, 125
Tying, 130–131

Unraveling, 30, 145

Verification of information, 20–21
Vertical integration, 4, 8–10
    acquisitions and sales of busi-
        nesses, 18–21
    asset ownership issues, 16–17
    asset specificity and, 8–13
    capital requirements and, 15–16
    costs of, 23–24
    information problems and, 13
    lowest cost alternatives and,
        13–14
    secure source of supply and, 15
    technological explanations for,
        14–15
Vishnay, Robert W., 93, 111

Wage increases within hierarchies,
    64–65
Warranties, 147, 154–158
Williamson, Oliver E., 22, 42, 69, 93,
    111, 174
Willig, Robert, 22, 42, 69, 133, 161,
    173
Winter, Ralph A., 133, 144
Woodward, Susan, 93

Zeckhauser, Richard J., 41, 68, 69,
    166, 173